I0438021

Promise Me

CHEROL MARTIN

authorHOUSE®

AuthorHouse™
1663 Liberty Drive
Bloomington, IN 47403
www.authorhouse.com
Phone: 1-800-839-8640

© 2010 Cherol Martin. All rights reserved.

No part of this book may be reproduced, stored in a retrieval system, or transmitted by any means without the written permission of the author.

First published by AuthorHouse 11/18/2010

ISBN: 978-1-4490-2041-5 (sc)
ISBN: 978-1-4567-1310-2 (e)

Printed in the United States of America

This book is printed on acid-free paper.

Certain stock imagery © Thinkstock.

Because of the dynamic nature of the Internet, any Web addresses or links contained in this book may have changed since publication and may no longer be valid. The views expressed in this work are solely those of the author and do not necessarily reflect the views of the publisher, and the publisher hereby disclaims any responsibility for them.

It was a beautiful Saturday afternoon. The wind blew fresh with the smell of spring flowers in the air, the sound of birds chirping, and the laughter of children playing. The noise of traffic was heard throughout the neighborhood, for the warmth of spring had finally arrived.

Sharay, Stephanie, and Marcie played double Dutch jump rope in front of Sharay's mother's house. The girls happily laughed as Stephanie and Marcie turned each rope for Sharay's turn to jump.

"Come on, Sharay, jump," the two girls yelled.

"Wait now," Sharay giggled, rocking back and forth and getting into position to jump into the ropes. Sharay watched carefully as the ropes whistled with a whirlwind sound through the air and struck the ground with the smack of a whip.

"I can get it this time," she told herself. Marcie and Stephanie turned the ropes faster and faster. Sharay took an ultimate chance and jumped into the whipping ropes. I'm going to make it, she thought hopefully. "I got it!" Sharay screamed, landing on both feet. "This rope has nothing on me," she sang, jumping, turning, and not missing one beat of the double-turning ropes. "Cause I'm as bad as Mohammed Ali."

"Sharay," Sharay's mother called softly, stepping out onto the front porch. "It's time for your lessons."

"Okay, Mama," Sharay answered, slowing down her jump as the girls slowed down the jump ropes. "I have to go," she told her friends while she wrapped the synthetic cloth around her soft-skinned hand. "Okay, Mama," Sharay answered, running up the porch steps of her Youngstown, Ohio home. "I'll see you later," she said, waving goodbye to her friends.

Sharay was a bubbly eight-year-old. She was to be lead singer for the junior choir on the following Sunday, something she had done since she could remember.

"I love you, Mama," Sharay said, looking up to her and holding her with one arm wrapped around her waist as they walked into the house.

"I love you too, Sharay, so much," her mother answered, kissing Sharay softly as they entered the dining room.

Sharay's mother sat down to the piano stool and instructed Sharay to breath. Sharay began to take deep breaths in and out as she twisted one of her four ponytails back together.

The closeness between Sharay and her mother could be felt throughout the room. Sharay, a brown-skinned angel, had a unique way of quieting a room with the tender melody of her voice. Sarah, Sharay's mother, continued to play each tune as she waited for Sharay to take a swallow of lemonade and position herself for rehearsal. Sarah gently nodded her head, and Sharay began to sing.

The sweet, mellow sound, coming from a small child, was astonishing to hear. Sarah, wanting Sharay to be in tune with each note, gave her child key points on how to lift her voice with strength and power, allowing the depth of breath to open up into an orchestra of song; she also taught her how to bring her voice down into a smooth tone, revealing precious tunes and harmonies.

While Sharay and her mother were rehearsing, the doorbell rang. Sharay hastily ran toward the front door.

"Sharay!" her mother called, taking larger steps than her daughter and trying to reach the door before she did. Sarah caught Sharay by the arm and reminded her of how dangerous it is for her to expose herself to possible harm.

"May I help you?" Sarah asked, running her finger over the chrome steel door knob, making sure that the door was locked.

"Well … yes," a man outside answered nervously, in a deep, scratchy voice. "I was looking for the Turner's place," he continued, removing his hat from his head.

"This is the Turners'," she replied, interrupting his sentence. "Oh— I'm sorry, how may I help you?"

"Yes, Ma'am, I just got into town, and I was trying to land myself a job at one of these big steel mills you got here, and, well … I was told you served good room and board."

"Oh, yes. Why thank you. Please forgive my manners; we were right in the middle of practice. Please come in."

"Yes, Ma'am, I'd be glad to," he answered, lifting up his worn dusty suitcase and wobbling from the weight of it. "I heard your singing when I first walked up the porch stairs; your voices are beautiful."

Sarah smiled, acknowledging his compliment. Sarah spoke as she guided the gentlemen toward the dining room. "Times are changing, and I'm trying to teach my daughter well, you know."

"Yes, Ma'am, I do, we have to be very careful these days."

Sarah turned to her daughter. "Sharay, I want you to go outside, but first could you please ask Mrs. Peters to come here?"

Mrs. Peters, one of Sarah's eldest workers, had worked for the Turner family for many years; she took care of making beds, helping with dinner, and some other different duties around the house that helped Sarah greatly. But in Sarah's eyes, she was more of a friend.

"You may rest your things here, sir," Sarah spoke, turning to the gentleman and extending her hand so they could kindly introduce themselves.

"Darin," he replied to her gesture, quickly wiping the sweat from the palm of his hands, "Darin Perez."

"It's a pleasure to meet you, Darin. My name is Sarah, Sarah Turner," she said, pulling her hand out of his.

"Nice to meet you as well," he respectfully replied.

Mrs. Peters entered the room and escorted their new houseguest to his quarters. After dinner and tucking Sharay into bed, Sarah quietly relaxed in the spare bedroom and thought of her husband, Mitch. *I'll be glad to see you, Mitch,* she thought while sipping on a cold glass of lemonade.

"Big Turner Mitch" was what many of the townspeople called him. Mitch Turner, a successful businessman, had diligently worked his business into a prosperous company called "Turn It Up Productions." Previous contracts and engagements had benefited the family enormously; to the top they had made it, and at the top was where they were going to stay. Mitch always had to travel from one state to another, looking for talent, which was something he was good at. However, the hard work had put a series of time spans between Mr. Turner and his wife. This was not new to Sarah, for this is how she met her husband of eight years. Sadly, the lonely days and nights were starting to take their toll. Mitch had recently called stating that there was a good possibility he would be home sometime this week.

I hope so, Mitch. How long can I continue to stay alone?

To pass much of the time, Sarah had opened their spacious home as a west-end hotel for whoever needed a place to stay. The Lord had truly blessed this family.

The next morning was as beautiful as the day before. The sun shone brightly into the home of the Turner family. Sarah walked down their long hallway with slippers and a housecoat on, holding her forehead and trying to wake up.

"Time to get up," Sarah stated, waking Sharay for church.

"Oh, Mama," Sharay mumbled inside her covers.

"Come on, Sharay," she said strengthening her tone as she pulled open the curtains. "We must be on time. How did you sleep, my beautiful princess?"

"Very well, thank you, my lovely queen," Sharay answered.

"Well ... let's get moving, baby; we don't want to be late."

"Okay, Mama," Sharay moaned.

"I'll see you downstairs." Sarah stood at the bedroom doorway.

"Okay, Mama," Sharay mumbled from under her sheets. "I'm getting up."

Sarah disappeared down the hallway to begin to get things ready for the day.

Sharay, not wanting to disappoint her mother, got up and began to get her things ready for church. *Oh I forgot to tell Mama about my dream,* she thought to herself.

As Sharay sat at the breakfast table, she began to tell her mother the strange dream she had had the previous night.

"Mama?"

"Yes, Sharay," her mother answered.

"Mama, I had the craziest dream last night. Stephanie, Marcie, and I were all sitting in this long hallway when a voice came to me and said that it had something to show me. But I could not see where this voice came from or who it was that was speaking. Then suddenly I was alone in another room filled with darkness. There was no one there but me, emptiness, and sadness. I could feel the sadness, Mama."

Sarah, who was preparing dinner early because of how busy Sunday always was, stopped preparing the meal and turned to Sharay, puzzled at the distance she could hear in her daughter's voice. She walked over to the kitchen table, pulled out a chair, and sat down so she could understand and comfort her child. Quietly she waited, allowing Sharay to finish telling the story of her dream.

"It was so sad, Mama."

"Are you okay, baby?"

"Yes, Mama, but it was so cold. Then this voice spoke to me, Mama," she began again as if to remember more of her dream. "It said, 'Follow me.' Oh—Mama, I was so scared that I fell upon my face. But a large shadow raised his hand while saying to me, 'Fear not, for I was sent to you; you must learn and understand.' Then I was turned toward the presence of the voice, and there before me were colors. They drifted toward me, pretty shades of blue, pink, red, and yellow; it was like a rainbow, Mama.

"The closer the colors came to me, the more they began to stretch out into long lengths of colorful scarves, and there were people there, Mama, holding the scarves. I began to follow the lengths of the scarves, which the people were holding, and the people danced, oh—how they danced, Mama, and their clothing was as pretty as the scarves."

Sharay got up from the kitchen table and began to act out the dancing, moving her arms from side to side in rhythm to an unheard beat. It was clear that merely remembering the dream had carried her away.

"And we went up and up, Mama. So high, the more I tried to reach the top, the further away the top was from me. I felt so good and free when, all of a sudden, I realized I was on a high cliff; the people around me were there too, stuck, Mama," Sharay began to cry. "They were bound, Mama, with chains on their ankles, crying and moaning to be freed. I screamed, 'Let me go!' But the man appeared to me dressed in deep, fearful black. 'You must pass by,' he said. I just screamed, Mama, and awoke."

"Oh … Sharay," her mother said, wrapping her arms strongly around her daughter to comfort her. "The Lord will let us know what it means. I know the dream scared you, but there is a reason why."

As Sharay and her mother embraced each other, Mr. Jess Cablow, their favorite houseguest, entered the room.

"Hey! What is going on in here?" Mr. Cablow said. "What cha' trying to do, scare the life out of this child?" he protested, pulling Sharay from Sarah's arms and wrapping one arm around her.

"Let me tell you, child, anybody who bothers you will have to answer to me." He raised his cane with the other arm. "You just tell them that old Jess said to bring it on."

Sharay began a giggle that turned into laughter as Jess raised that old cane of his. Jess was an eighty-eight-year-old man; he was short and had hair everywhere on his body except on his head. He had turned to Sarah after he lost his wife of fifty years.

Sunday morning was full of bustle for everyone. Breakfast and dinner had to be prepared. Sarah had to make sure each guest was cared for until she returned. Days like these made Sarah very thankful for having Mrs. Peters.

The church was unusually full. Many of the women wore their extreme headwear; it looked like a showcase of hats. There were many hats of style. Some of the hats sat high on one's head and others were more of a round shape, with fancy feathers stretching from the tips of their rims. Attention usually fell to people like Mrs. Rogers, a dedicated member of First Baptist Church, who was never late and always kind. Her hats always sat on her head with poise and posture.

As Sharay and her mother entered the church, many of the town's women greeted them, for they were well-known in the church house.

The ushers closed the church doors, letting the people know that it was time for silence. Sharay positioned herself to sing her song, with Sarah accompanying her on piano. The choir brought forth a collection of songs that were especially beautiful.

As the choir rested from their singing, Reverend Thomas stood and placed his Bible on the pulpit. "Praise the Lord," he proclaimed, and the congregation immediately responded, "Praise the Lord."

Again Reverend Thomas spoke: "Praise the Lord. Today the Lord has brought my attention to the relationship his people have with him." He paused, placing one hand on the Bible, turning his body toward the choir, and aiming his sight toward those behind him. "You know, the Lord consistently reminds us of the relationship he would like to have with his people, reminds us that he is a living God. He is a God who has heard your prayer and answered your request, a God of mercy, and a God full of judgment. He's our personal, saving God, the one and only Almighty God. If you will please," Rev. Thomas continued, "walk with me through the word of the Lord and turn your pages to Exodus, chapter twenty. We're going to follow the word of God."

The sound of turning pages began to flow through the church house. "Now, in reading this chapter, we find the Lord has opened a portion of his personality to us. He states, 'I, the Lord God, am a jealous God, visiting the iniquity of the fathers upon their children, unto thousands of them that love me and keep my commandments.' Now, let's take a moment and meditate on the words of the Lord. It seems the Lord is expressing some notion that he just might be visiting our land, our city. What will he find?" The reverend questioned the congregation, slapping his hand down on the pulpit. "Who is ready to stand before the Lord and his judgment?"

Quickly, the members of the church house realized that the reverend was not speaking to certain members of the church house, but to all who were attending the church house that day. He was telling everyone everywhere that each is accountable for his or her actions. Movement began in the church, and silence quickly became an utterance of grunts and sighs—a recognition that God Almighty was personally speaking to each of them.

"Now it seems," the Reverend concluded, "that the Lord is warning us of a visit from his judgment. Are you ready? We must focus our attention on why the Lord would set this passage in front of us this morning. Uh … surely it's for a purpose, meaning the Lord wants to talk to his children, settle some things. Maybe we've taken our blessings for granted. Let us reason with the Lord and bring ourselves to be humble and pray for his direction."

You could hear the members whisper while they gathered their belongings. "You know, Kelly," Sarah said, "Reverend really brought forth the message today."

"I know," answered Kelly. "It was a little scary, such a strong message. Well, I'm sorry, Sarah, but I really must get home. I have dinner in the oven, and Mark's parents are coming over for dinner. Call me." She threw her hand up as she walked away.

"Oh, that's all right, Kelly, I have quite a bit to do myself," Sarah said, fumbling with her purse. "Sharay," Sarah called. "Let's go, honey."

Sarah was dressed in a slender, olive green dress with matching shoes, hat, and gloves.

There was no question where Sharay's beauty came from.

"Sharay," Stephanie called, catching up to her.

"Can I, Mama?"

"Yes, baby." Sarah already knew Sharay wanted to go and play. "But make sure you change your clothes first."

"Yes, Mama; come on, Stephanie."

Sarah smiled, pulling her hat off and allowing the wind to blow through her long, bouncy hair. As Sarah continued to walk home, she watched the lovers across the street and it reminded her of her good days with Mitch; her thoughts drifted in the past. *May I have this dance?* she pictured Mitch asking her. Sarah softly glided across the floor. *Is this what you're looking for?* she had said, letting her sensual body flow into his waiting arms. *How long will I have to wait, Sarah?* he had asked as they continued dancing; *I'm hungry for you now.* Sarah could see him leaning forward passionately, kissing her.

"You shouldn't swing it like that, lady!" some young boys yelled as they drove by, shaking Sarah out of her thoughts.

"Mama, Mama!" Sharay yelled, running to her mother.

Sarah fearfully ran toward her daughter.

"Mama, Daddy's home."

The expression on Sarah's face changed as she looked up toward their house.

"Okay, baby," she said, giving a sigh of relief. "You just go with Stephanie and play, and don't you ever scare me like that again." As she walked up the porch stairs, she was still shaken up from Sharay's cry.

"Hey, baby," she said, throwing her hat over on the hallway chair. "How long have you been home?" Sarah asked as she walked into the kitchen, smiling at her long-missed husband and hoping he felt the same longing for her. Mitch, a tall, medium-built, dark-skinned man, turned while drinking a glass of lemonade.

"Actually, I just got in," he explained, swallowing quickly. "I see you took my baby to church today," he said staring at Sarah, looking her up and down.

"Well yeah, baby. You know how I love going to church and taking Sharay with me."

"What have you been doing since I've been gone?"

"Oh, you know, same old thing," she said as she slid each finger from her silky green gloves and dropped them onto the kitchen table. Disappointed that her husband had not captured her in a passion of love, Sarah quickly decided within herself that maybe Mitch had lost all of his love for her.

Mitch walked up to Sarah as she turned and reached for a glass. He leaned against her body, rubbing his hand down her thigh while taking in a deep breath and smelling her hair.

"Like always, baby, you smell so good to me. I missed you, Sarah." Mitch scooped down and picked Sarah up in his strong, masculine arms. "What am I going to do with you, you sweet, fine woman?"

Sarah lips melted as her husband's lips gently pressed against hers. "I love you baby," she said.

Just then, Sharay ran into the house. "Would you take me and my friends to get some ice cream, Daddy?"

"Oh … Sharay," he hesitated, not wanting to put Sarah down.

"Yes, Daddy," Sharay said, pulling Mitch's arm downward and insisting he put Sarah down and take her and her friends for ice cream.

"Well baby, I guess you have to give her some time too." Sarah whispered in Mitch's ear, sliding from out of his warm, comforting arms. "I'll be waiting here for you when you get back," Sarah revealed.

While Sharay and her father were out, Sarah continued with dinner and decided to invite a few friends over. "Are you sure you want to invite guests over, Sarah?" Mrs. Peters questioned. "You know it's been a long time since you've seen your husband."

"Well yeah, I know, but maybe it will spice the evening up just a little more. You know how Mitch enjoys a night of fun with family and friends," she said. Sarah dialed the number of her best friend, Angie, who quickly accepted the invitation, stating that she and her husband Frank would be delighted to come over.

While sitting at the dinner table, Frank, Marcie's dad, brought up in conversation the fact that Sharay and Marcie were trying out for the play that was coming to Youngstown.

"Oh ... ," Mitch said, looking at Sarah. He was puzzled because he had not heard the news yet.

"I'm sorry, baby; I was going to let you know." Sarah cut her eyes over to Frank. "I would have told you, honey, if given the opportunity."

"I apologize; I didn't mean to start any trouble," Frank said.

"Why did you have to bring that up, Frank? Now of all times," Angie replied.

"Truthfully, if my wife was a little more honest with me, I wouldn't have to hear family business from the neighbors," Mitch said.

"Please, honey, let's not make this bigger than it has to be," Sarah pleaded.

"Bigger?" Mitch threw down his napkin, "I guess it's real convenient for you not having me here at home."

"No, baby, you know how much I miss you." Sarah expressed, not wanting to upset her husband.

"Yeah, by overpowering everything I do and say. I said I did not want this child to sing; it's not enough that she sings in that money grabbing church of yours?" Mitch angrily expressed.

"Hey, man, why don't you just let this ride over? It's your night, man," Frank said. "You're home; it's your night," he continued, patting Mitch on the shoulder.

"Look, Frank, I don't need you telling me how to run my home or my wife."

"Hey, man," Frank responded, holding both of his hands up in defense.

"Mitch!" Sarah shouted.

"Mitch!" Angie called out, holding Sarah by her arm.

"I think it's time for us to go; come on, Angie," Frank said.

"I'll talk to you tomorrow," Angie said, not wanting to leave Sarah, but knowing that she would be out of place if she stayed.

Sarah nodded her head back and forth, embarrassed by her husband's actions.

"I'm sorry." Frank said, exiting the house.

"When is this play supposed to happen?" Mitch asked Sarah.

"The audition is tomorrow." Sarah answered softly as she began to clean up the dishes from the dining room table.

"Why would you allow this child to audition, when I told you I don't want her to sing at all?" Mitch yelled, frustrated and angry.

"Why would you allow another child to pursue a career and not help your own flesh and blood?" Sarah asked nervously.

Sharay eased her way to her mother's side.

"Go to your room, Sharay!" Mitch shouted.

"Dad," Sharay cried out.

"What did I tell you? Go to your room." Mitch's voice echoed.

"Mitch," Sarah responded, "you don't have to speak to her like that!"

Sharay could hear her mother and father arguing as she climbed the stairs.

"Don't you say another word, or I'll hurt you Sarah." He intensely grabbed her by the neck and tightened his grip as he pinned Sarah against the wall. "I'll hurt you, Sarah."

Sharay ran down the stairs and saw her father hitting and screaming at her mother.

"Get off of her!" she screamed, hitting and kicking her father. "What did we do? Get off of her." Her voice fell faint as she saw Sarah's eyes begin to close. "What did we do?"

Mitch took his hand from around Sarah's neck and Sarah dropped to the floor. He coldly walked into the living room and sat down on his favorite chair. "Come here Sharay," he demanded.

With fright in her eyes, she slowly obeyed her father's command. "Yes, Daddy?" she answered.

"You must understand," he began as Sharay knelt down beside her father, "I know what's best for you. Your mother is wrong." He laid his head on the back of the chair. "One day you'll be old enough to understand," he said as he fell asleep.

Sharay, frightened and confused by her father's words, backed away from him and ran to her mother's aide. "Are you all right, Mama?" she whispered, kneeling down beside her mother, afraid of waking Mitch. "We have to leave, Mama," she said hastily. "We have to go," she said as she tried to lift her mother from the floor to get her to run.

"Sharay," her mother moaned, with tears streaming down her face. "There's no place to go."

"Yes Mama; we'll run, Mama."

"No … Sharay," her mother answered. "There's no place to go."

"Yes, Mama," she insisted, "we'll run, and run, and run, Mama. Please, Mama, don't stay. He's going to hurt you."

Sarah took her precious baby's face into her trembling hands and shook her head no; she positioned herself back up on her feet and walked into the kitchen. "I need to put some things away," she said, dismayed about the incident that had just taken place. "Sharay, I want you to go upstairs to your room, and I'll be up to kiss you goodnight."

"Oh, Mama," Sharay cried, and she stomped up the stairs to bed.

Sarah, broken hearted, followed her up the stairs to Sharay's bedroom.

"You need any help, baby?" She leaned against the doorway.

"No, Mama. I'm sorry, Mama."

"I know, baby," she said, holding Sharay so tenderly in her arms.

"I'm so scared. He's going to hurt you; I know he is. How come he always has to come back?" Sharay asked, kneeling down for prayer; Sarah kneeled down beside her little girl. "I made a promise, Sharay, an undeserved promise."

Sarah returned downstairs after Sharay fell asleep. She tried to find some understanding of Mitch's actions. Sarah had worked so hard to turn this house into a home. Was it possible that all was lost, that everything had lost its meaning? Mitch began to squirm in his chair, so Sarah quickly removed herself from the kitchen and entered the spare bedroom. She was almost asleep when she felt her husband's warm body covering hers. "I'm sorry, baby," he said, running his hands through her hair. "I just go crazy," he said, shaking his head. "All I can think about is you. I don't know what I would do if someone touched you. You and Sharay are always together. I'm never here and have no part in anything."

"And you wonder why?" Sarah questioned. "You're not going to blame us just because you wanted to live out your dreams."

"Baby, you had dreams, didn't you?" Mitch thoughtlessly questioned.

"Yes, I had dreams. But what did you do? You came and took them away. 'I'll take care of you, Sarah. Please stay and take care of our daughter.' I did, and now you even want to take away her dreams. Well ... it won't happen, Mitch, not again. Get off of me," Sarah demanded angrily.

Mitch reluctantly removed himself from Sarah and lay next to her on the bed. "You won't have to worry about me anymore, Sarah; I'll be reporting back to New York tomorrow. You and Sharay can have one another."

Quietly the tears streamed down Sarah's face. The next morning, Mitch gathered his things and stormed out the front door with his suitcase in his hand; he was headed back to New York, giving no explanation for his behavior and no date when he would return.

New music groups were being discovered in every state: Earth, Wind and Fire; the Ohio Players; Marvelous Marvin Gaye, who returned from retirement; the Jackson Five; and the newcomer, Mr. Barry White, who had a style of his own that surged in women's hearts as he crooned with the sensual melody of his live orchestra.

Turn It Up Productions had also expanded tremendously. Youngstown had begun to expand with new talent. Bands such as Black and Free, Ebony Child, and Sweet Thunder were all anxious to meet with Mitch, trying to reach stardom. Everyone knew Turn It Up Productions was the place to go.

"Good morning, sir," Mitch's secretary said in greeting, surprised and unaware that Mitch had returned to New York. "I didn't expect you back so soon. I was going to leave these messages on your desk, but since you're here ... ," she said, extending her arm to hand Mitch the sheet of names. "Sir, they're the names of three bands wanting to meet with you. Are you all right?" she questioned, since Mitch seemed unaware of her presence. "Things didn't work out for you at home, again?" Donna was aware that Mitch had cancelled every appointment until the following week.

"Donna, that's none of your business," he selfishly answered, loosening his tie and sitting down in his king's chair, the chair that represented his empire. "Just set them on my desk," he advised, feeling smothered by her continued questions. Donna departed from Mitch's office and continued with her work.

What is wrong with me? Mitch asked himself. *All I want to do is love you, Sarah. What am I to do?* He pondered, puzzled, not knowing how to recover from the damage he had caused his family. Mitch turned to pity and whiskey to try and find the answer. Hours turned into days, days turned into weeks.

However, Sarah, so unselfishly, still held onto her husband.

"Hello, pumpkin. Did you have a good day at school?" Sarah asked Sharay back at home.

"Yes, Mama, I did."

"I have news, honey."

"What's that, Mama," she asked, feeling doubtful of what her mother had to say. "Is it good news?" Sharay asked, slumping down in the kitchen chair.

"Wait a minute, baby. Do you remember the play that came to Youngstown? Well … the production company has announced all over the radio station that they're having new auditions."

"What? Mama!" she shouted, jumping out of the chair.

"Yes, baby; somehow, I pray she gets better, but one of the main characters became ill, so announcements have gone out all over the radio: eight-year-old needed."

"That's me, Mama! That's me!" Sharay exclaimed, jumping up and down. "Thank you, Mama," she said, hugging and squeezing Sarah very tightly.

Sharay and Sarah timely arrived at the scheduled appointment time for auditions. Unsurprisingly, many of the town's talent had shown up for the auditions. Children and adults were excitedly conversing over the huge opportunity of being in the play, "Little Decker." Sharay was overwhelmed with the excitement of the many people there; some were standing around supporting family and friends and others were awaiting their great chance at fame. She carefully carried herself in a professional manner. Squeezing her mother's hand, she and Sarah positioned themselves in the standing line. After a twenty-minute wait, Sharay heard her name called. She answered nervously, "I'm Sharay."

"Come with me," the instructor informed her. "Are you here with Sharay?" the instructor asked, pointing to Sarah.

"Yes," Sarah answered. "I'm her mother."

"Stand with me." With pen and paper in his hand, he began to call out other names.

The names he called were Cherol, Falesha, Marcie, Tyra, and Stephanie. Three of the girls responded immediately, but there was no response from Marcie or Stephanie.

"Where are they?" Sharay pondered.

"I don't know," answered Sarah, her eyes scanning the grounds, hoping the children would show up.

Again, the instructor called the two unanswered names. "Last call," he stated.

"Hi. I'm Marcie," an out-of-breath child answered, running toward the instructor.

"I thought you weren't going to make it," Sharay said, releasing the uneasiness she was feeling.

"Don't feel bad, so did I. Where is Stephanie?" Marcie questioned.

"I don't know; her sister was supposed to bring her," Sharay answered.

The instructor called out the name of another girl who responded immediately. "I would like for all of you to follow me," he said, directing the children into a large gymnasium. "I am the first and the last person you will see leading this routine. I will show you one time and one time only, so please pay attention. If your name is called out, please go to your right, if not, thank you very much and I'm sure someone will need your talent soon. Good Luck."

Sitting ahead in the left-hand corner were three very quiet people who showed no signs of emotion. The instructor set his pen and paper down, and just as fast as he said "one, two, one, two, three," the music began to play and the instructor began to dance a routine that was smooth, timely, and perfected.

"Okay, that's it. It's your turn; line up."

The girls quickly lined up an arm's length apart and began: one, two, one, two, three. All the girls began to perform the dance routine as closely to what the instructor had shown them as possible.

"I'll take you, you, and you. Thank you very much; have a good day," the instructor said to the other girls whose names were not called. Both Marcie and Sharay began jumping up and down, for both were accepted into the play.

"Girls, girls. I would like for you to settle down," he said, moving his hands in a downward motion. "I have more news for you that you may not be aware of; there's an additional part needed, and actually, it is the greater of the parts. As you know, a request was sent out for an eight-year-old. Well, this part is for our lead singer. Is there any one of you who can sing?"

Sharay and Marcie quickly raised their hands. "Yes, we can."

The instructor called Sharay first and then Marcie. Both girls' voices rained out in sound, but Sharay was the one chosen. Excited and disappointed that she did not get the part, Marcie congratulated Sharay and Sarah, with Frank shaking Sarah's hand. "I don't know what it is about you Turners; you always seem to get the part."

The play went on for weeks. Amazed by the creative writers, fans rushed through the doors each night to see the irresistible play, "Little Decker." Stephanie was one of those fans anxious to see Little Decker and her friend's great performance. Disappointed about missing a far-reaching opportunity to perform, she was determined not to let her friend down. Stephanie was not a singer—Sharay and Marcie were—but she could really dance. She watched, bright-eyed as the dancers performed across the floor of Powers Auditorium.

"Little Decker" was fascinating. Its story was based on a ship built in the late eighteen hundreds, set aside and forgotten because of its deteriorated splendor. Little Decker yearned to be loved again. Docked at Virginia naval base, he watched many navel sailors walk past flexing their strength and might and never looking toward him, the old ship of doom. Somehow, it seemed everyone had forgotten that he was a patriot too, that he fought for the nation. In all his sorrow, Little Decker never gave up, believing one day he would be revived again.

That day did come, and Little Decker was needed. In a time of trouble, when the largest ship of the fleet was tossed to and fro in a terrifying storm with no one able to save its crew, Little Decker was called to duty. His old engines rumbled as the superior officers turned the ignition. With no time to lose, Little Decker pushed through the strong waters to save those stranded by the sea's power. Not only did he make it to the troubled crew, but Little Decker also brought them all back to safety. Women and children danced with joy and praise that Little Decker, the old ship of ruins, had returned again and saved their men from the dangers of the stormy waters.

The praises went out to Little Decker, the ship that saved so many, more than he could carry, and brought them home. In appreciation of Little Decker's triumph, he was restored. A large group of many, young and old, worked on the decks of Little Decker, buffing and shining until he was completely renewed. The audience applauded with pleasure and cheer, saying goodbye to "Little Decker" on its final night. The girls had given their best performances, and the little girl that was ill recovered. The play was over.

Mitch never knew of Sharay's performance. Once Mitch had left for New York, he never called home and never came home.

Sharay did not mention her father again; she escaped into summer fun, taking comfort in knowing her mother was always there. Nothing else seemed to matter except Marcie and Stephanie. On the other hand, Mitch had made his pity party into an extreme one. Donna, knowing the procedures and policies of the company, willingly carried on the duties of the business with hopes that Mitch would soon return to the company. New groups had jumped on board with Turn It Up Production, expanding the business even more. Wardrobe, scheduling appointments, and other business engagements were being piled onto the staff, and more and more help was needed. Donna had stretched her workload as far as she could go; she needed Mitch to get himself together and return to his company.

All right Mitch, if I have to come and get you, that's what I'll do, Donna thought to herself and proceeded out of the office. Knocking at Mitch's penthouse door, Donna anxiously waited for an answer. Again, she hammered on the door, waiting for an answer. Dressed in a two-piece, tailored white suit, she paced her strongly shaped legs back and forth at his penthouse door, needing Mitch to answer more than ever. Mitch was a businessman who was always on time; he had perfected his professionalism and always appeared educated, good-looking, and clean. He was the kind of man any woman would dream of having.

How could Sarah allow a fine man such as Mitch to destroy himself? Donna thought to herself as she reached under the doormat and pulled out the key to Mitch's penthouse door. Mitch had informed Donna that the key was hidden under his doormat, just in case of an emergency.

Donna pondered the key, thinking about the right thing to do. She planned to say, "You said in case of emergency, Mitch. Well, this is that emergency." Donna eased the slender gold key into the small penthouse keyhole. "Mitch," she cautiously called out, "Mitch are you here? I don't mean to intrude," she said, easing the door closed. "I really need to talk with you." Unexpectedly, Donna found no one and nothing; the penthouse was spotless, empty. Disappointed but not giving up hope,

Donna continued to search the rest of the penthouse. After looking in his bedroom and finding not one trace of Mitch, she slammed her purse to the floor, wondering, *What am I supposed to do now, Mitch?* Donna snatched her purse from the floor and opened the penthouse door. There, standing before her, were Mitch, in a drunken state, and two girls—one standing on either side of him. "Well, well, well," Mitch said. "I knew you would come for me."

"Come for you?" Donna furiously expressed.

"You see this young lady here?" Mitch said to the young ladies holding him up as he pointed at Donna, "she can fill both of your shoes."

The girls, both stunned at what Mitch had said, dropped his arms from their shoulders and went on their way, causing Mitch to fall directly into Donna's arms.

"Uh … Mitch," Donna responded, releasing the anxiety she felt from the weight of his body falling onto hers.

"I knew you would come," he whispered, trickling splattered particles of spit into her ear.

Donna, disgusted by the state of mind Mitch was in, pushed him off of her, causing him to stagger to the left side of the room.

"Okay, Donna," Mitch spoke as he tried to control his balance, "You … think you know what I need? Well, let me tell you," Mitch said, speaking in a drunken manner, "I can look at you and see exactly what you need."

Donna, not appreciative of Mitch's unkindly remark, stepped to Mitch and slapped him directly across the face. "Tell me what you see now, Mitch."

"Come on, Donna, give a brother a break." Mitch said, holding the side of his face.

"We don't have time for this, Mitch," she said, pulling his clothing off. "I'm taking you straight to the shower and you will swallow all the water you can and get yourself together."

"I knew you would come," Mitch said as Donna led his half-dressed body into the bathroom. Donna prepared the temperature of the water and Mitch gratefully stepped in.

"This is exactly what I need," Mitch mumbled, allowing the warm water to run down his back.

Donna closed the shower door, leaned her craving body against the outside of the shower door, and tried to pull herself together. She didn't want to reveal that she would love for Mitch to captivate her with the warmth of his steaming body. *The feel of your body next to mine, Oh Mitch, I remember.*

After a few cups of coffee, lots of rest, and a little play, Mitch and Donna were able to catch up on things concerning the office.

One of Donna's main concerns was about a new group that had jumped on board called Feel Me Baby. They would not stay in compliance with the company policies and refused to follow procedures.

Mitch and Donna both made it back to the office the following morning and began to run the company in an orderly fashion. One morning, not long after Mitch's return, the lead member of Feel Me Baby intruded into Mitch's office while he and Donna were going over the week's schedule.

"May I help you, Brian?" Donna asked; she was familiar with Brian's many rude, unscheduled visits.

"No, you may not," Brian harshly answered, stepping in between Donna and Mitch. "Are you Mitch?"

"Yes. I'm Mitch."

"Hold up." Donna said as she reacted, stepping back around Brain's large, round frame and wiggling her body in between the two men.

"Wait a minute, Donna, allow me to handle this," Mitch responded, wanting to stay professional.

"That is exactly what I'm talking about, Mitch. No appointment or call, you just think you can bring your fat behind in this office anytime it's convenient for you. I don't think so ..."

"Donna, I can handle this; allow me to, Donna," Mitch replied as he forced her out of his office.

"Okay, it's like this," Brian began to speak as Mitch tried to pull himself together from wrestling with Donna. "I don't know what kind of game you're trying to play, but I was told we would have a gig by now. What is it man?" He made some gestures with his hands. "I mean, by the looks of things, you seem to have yourself together, fine leather chairs," he rubbed one hand over the leather chair, "gold ink pens," he mocked, sitting on the top of Mitch's desk. "But where's mine?" he asked, tossing the pen onto Mitch's desk.

"Why don't you have a seat—in the chair, that is?" Mitch kindly chastised Brian. "I have to admit," Mitch began, "I do have some apologizing to do. I had a few personal problems that I normally don't let get in the way, but this time, man, they seemed to get me down. Now what's going on? Look, I'll do it like this, give me the name of your group and I'll ..."

"The name of my group, man that's crazy, you don't know our name. Let me put these sweet words in your ear, Mitch: if we don't have a gig within a week," Brian said strongly, "you'll be singing a song you never heard." Standing up from the soft leather chair, fixing his necktie, and flashing the diamond rings on his fingers, he walked out of the office.

Mitch was not frightened by Brian's threats, but felt it was his fault that such an angry group member had walked into his office. Now more than ever, he realized the stress he had put on his company and Donna.

Mitch called Donna into his office and apologized for the mess he had left her in. "Update me: what's the name of the group, the style of music? This is my fault," he expressed, holding his head in the palm of his hands.

Donna returned with all of Mitch's requests filled, and she slid the eight-track tape into the player and pushed play. The music coming from the player sounded like a schoolyard band playing in someone's garage. "What is this?" Mitch exclaimed. "Where did it come from?"

"I'm sorry, Mitch." Donna tried to explain, because it was her first time hearing them also. "I was so overwhelmed with work that I assigned some of the staff to go out and sign on contracts."

"Contract!" Mitch exclaimed, pounding his forehead in disbelief. "Don't tell me they have a contract?"

"Yes, Mitch, they have a contract," she answered distastefully after fumbling through some filed papers.

Silence filled the room. Mitch knew if he had not allowed his problems at home to get in the way of business, all of this probably would not have happened. But that didn't matter; Mitch knew Brian's undeveloped style of music could not go on his label. Something had to be done. Ignoring a situation was never Mitch's way of handling business, but at the time that was all he felt he could do until he thought of some way to get out of this contract. Speaking with other staff members and the young man who accepted Feel Me Baby as a fabulous group for the label, Mitch found out that Brian meant every word he said: his gangster ways were real; he was not the type of man to play around with. Brian was used to getting his way or taking it by whatever means were necessary. The only problem was that legally, Brian was right.

Mitch and Donna continued to ignore Brian, surprised they did not hear from him the next week as he had threatened they would. They both continued on with their office duties. Donna and Mitch's relationship grew stronger. The time they shared together strengthened their trust and interest in one another. On both a work and personal level, they were a team. For weeks, the company moved forward, with Mitch jumping back on his feet and Donna right at his side. Still even more groups joined the production company of the Turner family, and its prosperity had never been greater. Mistakenly, both he and Donna foolishly ignored the threats of Feel Me Baby.

Spring had bloomed across the land, leaving traces of her beauty everywhere, but summer's heat had also come. The earth thirsted for rain. Jess and Mrs. Peters sat on the front porch drinking ice-cold lemonade, enjoying the day, while Sarah soaked her garden with water to keep her precious flowers from withering in the heat.

"How do you do it?" Darin asked.

"Do what?" Sarah questioned.

"You know, keep yourself so together," Darin continued, standing over Sarah, who had kneeled down to pick the weeds from her garden. "Faithful Sarah, do you ever complain?"

"Oh … don't tell me you're worried about me, Darin; what about you?" she asked, standing up and facing Darin. "You're the one getting burned almost every time you go to that old hot blast furnace."

"There's no joke in that; I thought I was going to have to come to you again last night."

"Last night. Why? What happened last night?" Sarah asked.

"Promise not to panic," he said, raising his shirt.

"Oh my goodness," Sarah exclaimed, dropping the water hose and splashing the water onto Darin's face.

"I'm sorry," Sarah apologized.

"No, you're not," Darin quickly replied, "you're beautiful. It's ok; I told you not to panic, Sarah. As fast as the coals were being thrown into that old furnace, the hot flames were bursting out; I couldn't help but get burned."

"Come in the house, Darin, so I can put something on those wounds," Sarah said quickly.

"Young love," Mrs. Peters said.

"Yeah, young love that can get you killed," Jess replied.

"Well, what do you want her to do? She's not getting any love around here." Mrs. Peter's spoke sharply, turning her head toward Jess.

"I want her to do what she's been doing," Jess sternly replied.

"What, die a slow death? The child ain't done nothing but smiled. Let her have some fun!" Mrs. Peter's challenged him.

"Oh girl, do you remember how it was when we were young and love was new? The music was unbelievable," Jess expressed. "To be able to take your girl out and hear all of the famous people who used to come to town singing jazz and blues: Louis Armstrong, Ray Charles, and Nat King Cole; and let's not leave out hearing the Rat Pack would be coming into town. Frankie and the boys, what better time could you have?" Jess asked.

"Yeah, the ballroom in Idora Park was the place, wasn't it?" Mrs. Peters reminisced.

"Sure was. That would be the night of nights: police officers used their bright flashlights to direct traffic; car horns loudly blew, wanting the excited crowd to hurry out of the way. Boy ... you could hear the women's shoe heels clicking on the pavement, click, click," Jess said in imitation. "Boy, how they scurried, wanting to be first in line to hear Frankie sing. And the dancing, my goodness. Boy, how they danced: the swing, the cha-cha." Jess stood up and began to dance. "Did we dance or what? Come on girl let's show them what it's about," Jess persisted as he continued to dance.

"Show who? Man … sit your old self down before you get hurt," Mrs. Peters responded.

"Mama," Sharay called, running up the porch stairs.

"Come on, Sharay, let's show the old girl how to do it," Jess requested, wanting Sharay to dance with him.

"Sharay, did you call me?" Sarah asked, standing partially between the brick house in the screen door while watching Sharay and Jess cha cha.

"Yes, Mama. I wanted to know if it was all right to go to the park with Marcie and Stephanie." Sharay giggled as she continued her dance with Jess.

After receiving permission to go to the park, Sharay, Marcie and Stephanie began their journey.

"Sharay."

"Yeah, Marcie."

"Have you noticed the car that sits across the street from your mother's house?"

"Yeah, Marcie, I have."

"I wonder what they're doing there," Marcie pondered.

"I don't know, but have you noticed the man that sits in the back seat?" Sharay questioned.

"Yeah, I have." Marcie answered.

"Let's go see what they want," Stephanie said.

"No, Stephanie," grabbing her by the arm, "Mama said never talk to strangers."

Not wanting the men to acknowledge them, they swiftly jumped onto their bikes and soon were lost in summer fun. The three girls, all with ten speeds alike, loved to race their bikes around the winding roads that led through Mill Creek Park. There was so much to do there. The girls would skip rocks and watch the ducks race with their wings spread wide or ride the water like powerful motor boats until they reached their destination. At other times, the girls would go to the flower garden and count the many rows of flowers. The flower garden was often used for weddings too. Parents enjoyed taking their children to the park for picnics, fishing, or just to visit the fish pond.

While the girls enjoyed meandering alongside this beauty, a pack of boys were following their adventure along the waterfall and taking the deepest possible dives into the water. Each of the boys took his turn to jump into the flowing waters. The competition was especially pitched after they saw the girls watching excitedly and tensely; it was the best time for the young boys to show off. It was truly a dangerous adventure, for the boys did not know where they would land. They showed no fear in diving into the deep waters. The water splashed against the nugget-shaped, sharp-edged rocks as the boys continued to jump in. While watching the bravery of these boys, Marcie noticed a blue Buick slowly drive by.

"Sharay," Marcie said, nudging her, "Isn't that the blue car?"

"Yeah, it is. What is it doing down here?" Sharay questioned.

"Let's go find out." Stephanie said.

"No!" Marcie reacted, "let's go tell our moms!"

"Yeah," Sharay and Marcie repeated one after the other.

The girls hastily jumped on their ten speeds, fearful that the car was in the park at the same place as them. They frantically raced down the park's hill and around each curve.

"Come on, Sharay!" Marcie and Stephanie yelled, pumping the steepest hill before reaching Sharay's house.

"I'm coming, wait!" Sharay said, standing up on her bike peddles to give more speed to each turn of the bike's axle.

"I'm going to tell my dad," Stephanie yelled, gliding down the hill and turning her bike wheels toward her house.

"Mama," Sharay called out, anxious to tell her mother what they had seen, "Mama."

Sharay called out again. Sharay and Marcie ran though the hallway leading to the kitchen, "Mama," she called out, expecting to hear her mother's response by now. "Mama, where are you?" Sharay and Marcie ran through the doorway of the kitchen and found Sarah lying on the kitchen floor. "Mama!" Sharay cried out. She was horrified by the blood she saw surrounding Sarah's body. "Mama!" she cried, almost in a whisper as she dropped to the floor. "Mama, what happened?" she said, lifting her mother's lifeless body up to hers and rocking it back and forth. She was terrified of what she saw surrounding her mother. "Oh my God, Mama," she screamed.

"Oh my God!" Marcie cried out, slipping and falling into the blood surrounding Sarah. Marcie swiftly backed away from Sarah and tried to pull Sharay with her. Unable to make Sharay leave, Marcie ran for help. "Help! Help! Help! Mrs. Sarah!"

Angie and Frank heard the frantic cry of their daughter and ran hastily to find out what was wrong with her.

"Help!" she barely whispered, pointing toward Sarah's house.

"What, Marcie? What is it?" Angie shuddered as she swiftly checked Marcie's body because of the blood that was all over her.

"Help Mrs. Sarah," Marcie uttered, trying to bring the chilling words into an utterance of sound.

Frank immediately ran to the Turner's house as he yelled out to Angie to call the police.

Entering the Turner's home, Frank could hear the whimpering cry of Sharay. Recognizing his presence, Sharay looked up at Frank, who was rendered speechless by what he saw. "My Mama," she said, holding Sarah in her arms. "Please help my Mama," she cried, with tears streaming down her face. Frank took cautious steps toward Sharay, not wanting to slip in the blood that flowed from Sarah. It was obvious that she had been wounded badly. He kneeled down in front of Sharay and began to examine Sarah. Tenderly, Frank asked Sharay to leave the room with him. Sharay, not wanting to leave her mother, shook her head no, refusing. She tightly gripped Sarah and brought her body to a warm, comforting hold. "No," she said, "I won't leave my Mama."

Frank lifted Sharay's blood-soaked body and began to move her away from Sarah's badly beaten body. Restraining Sharay, he gently rested Sarah's body down on the floor. The horrific screams distressed the hearts of others as they watched Sharay's body stretched out in terrifying pain for the loss of her precious mother. "Don't leave me, Mama," she cried out as Frank carried her away from the awful scene.

Mitch rushed home after hearing the horrifying news of his wife's brutal death. Panic, anger and confusion haunted his mind. *I should have been there. Oh God! My baby, if I could only take it back,* Mitch thought. Mitch's quickness to overpower and control had initiated fear in his heart. *What would people think?* Upon arrival at the Turners' place, sadness filled his heart; almost immobile with what he would possibly have to face and endure. His knees quivered with fear. His heart raced and pounded like the beat of a drum. Wishing he could turn and run, he uttered, "Oh God, Sarah." The words quivered on his lips. He dropped to his knees. The officer gently re-covered her body with the once-white sheet, now blood-soaked from Sarah's beaten body. Uncontrollable tears rolled down Mitch's face in agony as he thought of the love he had lost. Now Sarah could never hear him say, "I'm sorry." Guilt began to scatter his mind, and with nothing left to do, he cried out her name and ripped his clothes in half.

Angie, recognizing Mitch, greeted him as he left the crime scene.

"Where is Sharay?" Mitch questioned, grievously concerned for the welfare of his precious daughter.

At the sight of Sharay, Mitch knelt down, tenderly opening his arms and expecting to find comfort in their embrace. He wanted nothing more than to protect his daughter from the terror that had invaded their home. Instead, he found an enraged, angry, accusing child. "How could you?" she wept. "My Mama!" she cried, ripping her nails into the side of his face.

"Sharay," Frank yelled as he restrained Sharay and took her into the house. Mitch stepped back onto his feet, astonished about the response he had received from his pain-stricken daughter. Angie embraced Mitch and gently escorted him to her house.

"Allow me to fix you a cup of coffee," Angie said, trying to find a way to assist Mitch.

"What am I to do?" Mitch whimpered. "My God," he said, unable to settle his emotions.

As he spoke those words, two officers from the Youngstown Police Department knocked at the kitchen door.

"Hello," they said as they approached. "May we come in?"

"Yes," Angie appropriately answered.

As they entered the house, the elderly, gray haired officer directed his questions at Mitch. "I understand you're the victim's husband?" he said.

Mitch looked up, realizing the officer was directing his questions to him. "Yes, I am," Mitch answered.

"I apologize, I know this is not a good time, but we need to ask you a few questions," the officer explained.

"Sure," Mitch responded, willing to render any help possible.

"Did your wife have any enemies? Do you know of anyone who would want to harm your wife?"

"No," Mitch answered, breaking down, teary-eyed.

"You have your own company, don't you? I am correct?" the officer asked as he proceeded.

"Yes," Mitch answered, "Turn It Up Productions, and no … I can't think of anyone who would want to harm my wife." He expressed this as he reached up and touched his face, for his salty tears were burning the scratches Sharay had deeply embedded in his skin.

"A fight with the cat?" the gray-haired officer questioned.

"My daughter … she's very upset," Mitch said, trying to explain.

"And what about your hands; did she also bust up your hands like that?"

"No, sir," Mitch responded defensively. "Last night … man … I was jumped. Oh I forgot all about this. Two men, they jumped me, they tried to rob me. I had to fight."

"Ummm," the officer stated.

"Did you report this incident?" the officer continued.

Mitch dropped his head, "No, I did not."

"Look, my name is Officer Brown, and this here is Officer Hopkins. We're the two officers who will be working on your wife's case."

"Sarah," Mitch said, "her name was Sarah."

"Sarah," the officer repeated respectfully. "I am sorry for your loss, Mr. Turner."

Each day became more uncomfortable for Mitch. Confounded and confused, he could not understand why anyone would want to hurt his precious wife. He tried to answer the questions he was asked, but the Youngstown Police Department had their doubts. Mitch cried tears of despair, expressed of pain, and made a lot of effort trying to comfort his unbelieving child, but the bruised and broken skin on his knuckles gave Y.P.D. a totally different view of this financially powerful man. Maybe Sarah was in his way. There was no forced entry into the Turner home, and no one saw anything strange or suspicious around their home other than the blue car that sat across the street. Mitch had stated that he was attacked the night before by two unknown men who had tried to rob him, but with no evidence and no one to verify his alibi; Mitch had become the Youngstown Police Department's number one suspect.

Later, after speaking with neighbors, boarders, and friends who had witnessed some of the abuse and neglect Mitch had given his family, Mitch was quickly arrested and charged with the murder of Sarah Turner.

The death of Sarah rippled through the community. Radio and television sadly announced the death of the town's very own songstress. Unknown to Sharay, Sarah was a famous jazz and blues singer. She had hidden this from her daughter for reasons now only known to Mitch. Famous producers, musicians, and singers all came to say farewell to their beloved Sarah.

A few days after saying goodbye to Sarah, Mrs. Peters tried to bring some understanding to Sharay concerning her mother's famous past. "I remember the first time I seen your mother perform," Mrs. Peters said, rocking Sharay, who was cradled in her arms of wisdom. "The curtains opened, showing only a wooden table with a red silky scarf draped across it. On the top of the scarf sat a radio that played soft music. Then she stepped out from behind the curtain, a beautiful female dressed in a red silky gown that followed every curve of her shapely body. When she opened her mouth to sing, the voice of a strong songstress came out. The feeling and mood she set quieted the whole ballroom. That's right, she sang at the ballroom right over there in Idora Park.

"Your mother was unique. Jazz and blues had been heard here many times before, but the flow of her voice was outstanding. When she finished singing, everyone stood on their feet and applauded wildly. I'm so sorry for your loss, Sharay; she can never be replaced."

Angie and Frank did everything they could to comfort Sharay and Marcie. Mitch was no longer able to run his own company; he transferred everything over to Sharay, placing Frank and Angie as overseers of her estate until her twenty-first birthday. Angie prayed for a way to relieve the pain that burned inside Sharay; nothing seemed to give comfort to her. After pondering and discussing things with Frank, they both decided it was best for Sharay and Marcie to change environments. Excited about their decision, Angie rushed up the stairs to tell Sharay the news. Opening the bedroom door, she found Sharay missing. Angie sat on the side of the bed, not knowing what to do, when she found a letter Sharay had written. The letter said: "The words I need to speak to you, Mama, almost seem unbearable to say. I search my heart to express the emptiness I feel each day yearning for you, wanting you here with me. The reverend said it is selfish not to let you go. I don't like him anymore, Mama. God wouldn't say that. I'm going to stop singing for him, Mama. I think the Lord is tired of hearing my voice, Mama. He has you and left me all alone. Isn't that selfish? All the people he already has and he took you, Mama, and left me all alone."

Angie knew then more than ever that she had to do something to free this child from her pain. Whimpers of tears sounded from under the closet door. It was Sharay; she was lying there, fading away into her last thoughts. Angie rushed Sharay to the hospital, praying for help, for the Lord to please come. Hours passed; Angie and Marcie sat hoping that no harm had come to Sharay. The poison she had taken was strong, and no one knew exactly how long Sharay was unconscious. The doctors were not able to wake Sharay; the nursing staff monitored her carefully. No one would be able to determine her condition until she was conscious again. Angie, overwhelmed with fright, questioned herself. She had taken on such a heavy task; could she carry this burden for her precious friend? Encouraged by the doctors, she sat and talked to Sharay to allow her to hear her and Marcie's voices as they said how important Sharay is to them. Marcie and Angie went to her beside. Everything within Angie told her that she had to make contact with Mitch; he had every right to be a part of his child's life.

Marcie slowly walked to Sharay's bedside, wanting nothing more than for Sharay to open her eyes, speak to her, and tell her that she was okay. She was her best friend. From an early age, all she remembered was her friend Sharay. Needing her friend, she leaned forward, gently squeezed Sharay's hand, and sang softly into her ear. "Jesus loves you, this I know; please don't leave." Sharay's little innocent hand tightened around Marcie's as tears streamed down both their faces. From that point on, they promised one another neither one would ever leave the other. They even brought Stephanie in on their promise—true sisters, from their hearts and in their blood.

Joy raced through Angie when she saw that Sharay was okay. Angie had decided that if she returned to work it might be a little too much for the girls, and so she decided she needed to take time off from her job as a school teacher. She began her daily routine of just being a mom.

The girls' new school was exciting and fun. Many opportunities were offered at Lincoln Junior High. The girls had finally made it to their teens, and the best thing was happening—a party. One of their new friends was turning thirteen and was having a huge birthday party, inviting all of her friends from school. She was very popular, so this meant everyone would be there. Marcie, Sharay, and Stephanie were anxious to get new outfits for the party. Angie, who was excited for the girls, raced downtown to help each one find her special outfit.

The city lights were bright with glamour. People walked the streets of downtown Youngstown, going in and out of the many stores: Strouss, Mckelvies, Livingston's, Silverman's, they were all stores of elegance. Just going downtown revealed an array of beauty. The city's steel industry had blessed this town; it was a town of blue-color workers. The smell of burning coals was everywhere, and smoke-filtered clouds circled the sky of the city, especially on the east side of town. Every time Angie had to take the girls to school, even though it was just a few miles away, you could smell the odor. But that never bothered the elders of the city. When the children would complain of how bad the odor smelled, the adults would say, "You ought to think God for that smell. That odor bought your dinner last night."

Sharay, Stephanie, and Marcie were very excited and a bit nervous. They could not believe there were so many clothes to choose from. It was their very first party as teenagers, and they wanted to look their best. Each girl tried on different outfits until finally they each found the one that was perfect.

The girls attended the party and met new friends. There were both boys and girls at the party, the girls had seen some of their faces before, but had never spoken to any of them. But now they were being introduced and learning their names first hand. It was fun hearing compliments on their pretty dresses, especially from the boys. How great it felt to be a part of the group and to now really know everyone's name. Everyone was so nice, and they were able to dance the whole time.

But things changed quickly after that night. Monday morning came in and brought the cloud of doom with it. The *Youngstown Daily* and the radio both reported that five thousand men had permanently lost their jobs. Without any notice or warning, on September 19, 1977, Youngstown Sheet and Tube was closing. The reports stated that the powerful steel mill would be transferring its main office to Chicago, Illinois, and it was unsure of how many more workers would be laid off. Men and women alike, who had packed their tin lunch boxes, were returning home in gloom, numb, not yet able to swallow the news they couldn't believe. "The decision will not only wipe out the jobs of about five thousand Youngstown area employees, many with thirty to forty years of service, but will indirectly end or affect many thousands of other northern Ohio jobs—those of railroad workers, truckers, scrapyard workers, and miners." The mayor of Youngstown said this as he tried to pull the city together.

A bomb had been dropped on Youngstown; how could anyone fight for the recovery of the city? They were unable to fight with picket lines because the plant was closing. The people felt that the government had left them hopeless. The new president of the steel industry had just announced, not even two months before, that the city had nothing to worry about; even with the changes in the steel industry, this giant corporation would be able to sustain. "Hundreds of steelworkers walked across the footbridge that separated the mill from the clock house and threw their hard hats and metatarsal shoes—the symbols of their trade—into the Mahoning River," stated the Youngstown news. "The scene which was broadcast on the National news may be an omen of the anguish to come. They called that day Black Monday." Children sat at their school desks, mothers and fathers sat at the breakfast table, and everyone listened as they reporters tried to explain why the steel corporations felt it was best to shut down.

How was this community going to survive this terrible flight? Who could understand how such a thing could happen to this blessed city, when even the most devastating storms would pass over the valley? Not this time; they were caught in a storm, a storm of despair. Jess was right, thought Sharay, and so was the Pastor. A storm had finally hit the Valley, and it was a bad one. "What is going to happen now?" Sharay questioned, not really knowing the ramifications of the question she had asked.

Stephanie suffered from the closing of Sheet and Tube more than any of the girls. Sharay and Marcie were able to fall back on the support of Turn it Up Productions. Frank had worked back and forth with the company at full strength. The transition was easy for Frank; he returned to New York and continued with the company's business. For Stephanie's father, it was a totally different story. With little education, and the majority of Youngstown in distress, there was no place to find a job, and if one was found, the salary was so low that a week's work only paid the rent. What was he to do?

Organizations were set up; the town's people knew more than ever that they had to work together. Many wanted to believe the stories of repair. They asked themselves, "What can we do to bring this city back together?" But so many others had lost hope. "How could they just transfer the company and leave us in such despair?" The effects of this closing hurt many steel mill workers. People scrambled to find their way, but fear was set in the hearts of many. Some went to church to pray, others left town, and others chose the only way they saw out. Sharay and Marcie could see the change in Stephanie; more and more they had to ask her to be a part of their sisterhood. Stephanie was feeling second; she no longer felt she was able to measure up to the adequacy of her friends.

She knew within herself that they loved her with all of their hearts and that there was no difference between them, but she still felt she had to depend on them for everything. Money was needed, and she was going to find a way to help her father. Sharay had made several failed requests to Frank to allow her and the girls to begin their singing careers with Turn it Up Productions. After all, it was her company, and her friend was in trouble. But Frank consistently refused. The answer was "No!" But why? His motives to refuse seemed just a little odd. Was he so out of touch with Sharay that he truly wanted to follow the ways of Mitch? When he so graciously expressed that he did not agree with the actions Mitch had taken against his family, Sharay and Marcie again began to hope. They believed the day would soon come when they would be recognized. But as for Stephanie, it was much harder. The days of need began to outweigh the days of want. Her family was failing.

Well, hard times came again; in 1981, Youngstown Corporations announced the shutdown of two other steel mills. Republic Steel and Brier Hill were both shutting down. The city was in grave distress; it had never recovered from the shutdown of Sheet and Tube, and now it was faced with more lost jobs. People asked themselves, "What do they want us to do?" All the people of the town became weary in their judgments. The city had collapsed. There was no hope and no trust. Was this the end of Youngstown?

The Valley was in deep trouble; it was now a city of desperation. Echoes of lost hope surrounded its borders. The ghostly smoke that once represented an industry of prosperity now left in the mind's imagination the impressions of a deserted ghost town. It was rumored that Youngstown was doomed. *How could we ever survive?* "Save Our City" groups marched to the state capitol. Candidates running for president visited the city and promised hope, but this only angered the citizens. Youngstown Public Schools stated that the school district was declining, that the city was out of money. Herds of families began to move to other states or suburbs, running from decades of fallen buildings that revealed the city's poverty.

By now, with all the hardship that was revolving around the city and Stephanie's family, their financial need could not be ignored any longer. Angie had listened to the girls' request again, and she knew that their idea to perform their own play to raise money for Stephanie was an excellent ideal. Angie had surrounded herself with the girls and felt she knew pretty much what was going on in their lives. So she spoke with Frank, demanding an answer to his consistent refusal to the girl's request and making known to him that the only reason their lives were on easy street was because of Mitch company. She also reminded him that the company really belonged to Sharay. Well, their request was answered, bringing the girls much happiness. So rehearsal for the play began.

This play was based on the story of three young girls who loved to sing and wanted to start their own singing group. Two of them had beautiful voices, but the third had a terrible sound to her un-tuned voice. But the desire was in her heart to sing. She prayed every night for the Lord to bless her with a beautiful voice like the others. "Oh Lord," she prayed, "if I could only sing." Her mother heard her constant plea and felt heartbroken that her daughter could not sing. She knew of a great teacher who had taught many to sing; many of this teacher's students had gone on to great stardom. So off her mother went to ask the skilled teacher to teach her precious daughter to sing. Which, with no delay, the teacher agreed to do. The teacher sat down at the piano stool and began to play, flowing her skilled fingers over each note she wanted the young girl to sing. "Now come on child, allow me to hear you sing." The young girl opened her mouth to sing and a screeching sound seemed to tumble from her lips. The teacher stopped her playing as her fingers stumbled over the keys. "My child," she said. "Are you ok?" she questioned.

"Yes," the little girl happily replied.

"Well, let's go over this again. Now listen very carefully. I want you to sing each note in tune with what I am playing." The young girl answered with cheer while the teacher positioned her large breast back into place. Again, she began to play the notes she wanted the young girl to sing, and again the girls screeching voice almost threw the teacher off of the piano stool.

"Wait right here," the discouraged teacher replied. She stepped to the next room, confronting the young girl's mother, who was awaiting her daughter. "My God, did you know your daughter could not sing?" she asked.

"Yes, I did," the little girl's mother answered.

"Well, Ma'am, why did you bring her to me?"

"That is exactly why I brought her to you; you're a great teacher."

"Well, I thank you for your glory," the teacher replied, "but I am not God. This child cannot sing."

"Oh please," the mother hopelessly begged, "I've been able to give my daughter anything she's ever needed, but this thing I cannot give."

"Now look," the teacher sternly replied, "there are some things in life we cannot have; you are doing your child no justice by convincing her she will be able to sing."

"But I can buy a little time, until she's old enough to understand," she said, flashing many dollar bills in the teacher face. The moment was not a good one for the teacher, and she fell to the temptation. After many weeks of trying to teach the young girl to sing, the teacher grew weary of her screeching voice. She began to think of a way to get out of the terrible deal. So early one morning, without further adieu, she raced to Satan, the wicked one.

"So ... you want me to take this child's life because she wants to sing?" the wicked one questioned.

"Yes," she begged. "Yes, please," the teacher cried out.

"Well, that's not fair," he said. "Even I like to sing. I like to wiggle my figure," the wicked one said, smoothly moving and wiggling his body. "Let's do a great thing; there is one I know who is greater than I, and he has heard the little one's request and is ready to answer her with a great gift of voice. See, you came to the wrong one, but since you're here ... ," and they began to whisper so no one would hear the trickery that was about to be set before the young girl and that could cause her to lose her new gift of song.

When the little girl prayed again, very earnestly, an angel came to her with a whistling sound of wind and told her that she had to pass a test, that the Lord had a great blessing for her and that he would be with her. The angel also said that an evil one had set a trap for her. All she had to do was make a choice. The young girl had to choose which style of music she would like to sing, and only her heart would reveal the truth.

The girls went through each character's part, checking to see who wanted to play what part. Stephanie was chosen to play the little girl who could not sing, because the play was written especially for her. The girls asked Angie if she would play the part of the teacher, and she agreed. Laughter filled the house as Angie and the girls put together the play. The young girl's choice would be revealed through a sing off. Her heart would make the choice between gospel music and soulful, heart-filled music.

Stephanie was extremely happy about the hard work her friends had put into making this play a success. Angie had become a core part of the girl's life, actually forgetting about her own. Which Marcie didn't seem to have a problem letting Angie know that she was becoming too involved in the girl's life.

It was graduation time. The girls had successfully finished high school and were about to make their first steps onto life's path as adults; the principal reminded them of this at commencement. Angie sat happily watching the girls as each one crossed the stage when their names was called. Her heart also mourned the loss of her friend Sarah, who she knew would have been sitting beside her with the same feelings of accomplishment and joy. Instead, there she was again, sitting alone through all the girls' achievements. Frank had taken on the business of Mitch and lost all track of his own family. His name was only repeated through the house as one who once lived there. Angie had learned the desolation of the pain her friend Sarah had suffered before her death. The caps flew up in the air, and there it was: the girls had achieved their first triumph of life.

After returning home, Angie proudly climbed the stairs with a tray of lemonade to celebrate with the girls their great triumph, but upon entering the room, she heard Marcie say that she would not be entering college. Stunned at Marcie's confidence, she confronted her. "What do you mean you will not be entering college Marcie?"

"You heard me, mother," she replied, realizing her mother had heard her conversation but not willing to acknowledge Angie with the respect she deserved.

"That's right, mother; since you took it upon yourself to butt into my conversation, I guess I'll let you know now. I will not be attending college. And I am going to New York with Dad."

"What! You're what?" Angie asked.

"You heard me, mother," she answered, approaching Angie angrily, as if she would hit her if she had to.

Sharay jumped off of the bed and stood in between Marcie and her mother. "What is wrong with you, Marcie?"

"That's right, defend her, that's all you two do is stand up for one another anyway. Well, I'm sick of you," Marcie said angrily.

Angie's body gave up its strength and fell to the floor, but Sharay caught her and sat her down on the bed.

"What is wrong with you?" Sharay boldly asked, "That's your mother."

"No. That's your mother, and you can have her," Marcie said to Sharay, swollen and ready for a fight, "unless you want to miss this fantastic opportunity that my dad has set up for us," she said, cunningly changing her tone. "We're going to New York, all of us."

"All of us?" Stephanie inquired, jumping to her feet with desire and excitement.

"All of us," Marcie answered, speaking with authority.

Stephanie quickly joined sides with Marcie.

"I figured you would come. Umm, I think that completes everything needed to make sure Angie will be here all alone, just like she left me," Marcie said conclusively.

"What are you talking about, Marcie? I've never left you."

Marcie looked down at Angie, and then she just ignored her with anger beaming from every part of her body.

"What is wrong with you?" Sharay asked.

"Sharay, remember your promise. Remember that we said we would never leave one another, blood sister. Let's go," she demanded. "My father has our tickets waiting for us at the airport."

"Stephanie, I can't believe you're going for this," Sharay said, questioning her conscience.

"I'm sorry, Mrs. Angie, but my family's been hungry a long time; maybe I can help my father," Stephanie said.

"Oh … you're coming too, Sharay, poor little broken-hearted Sharay," Marcie taunted. "You're coming; you promised!"

Pain rippled through Angie. She had experienced deceit and trickery in the worst way, by and through the ones who she thought loved her the most. The desertion she felt in her husband's actions grieved her soul. Frank's loyalty to his family had long been tarnished by his actions toward Angie. Questions of infidelity and lies had become a strong part of their relationship since the death of Sarah. *What could I have done for you to treat me so wickedly?* her mind pondered. "Why? Why would Marcie go alone with him? I love them, I loved them both. Oh my God," she cried out, "Help me, help me, my baby."

Angie spent days crying and begging the Lord to give her answers.

She knew she had to do something to get her daughter back. It wasn't as if she didn't know where she was or who had her. The core of Frank's actions with Marcie was in strong question; trying to find answers regarding Frank's motivations overpowered Angie. She knew she had to get up, stand up, and fight for what belonged to her. *The girls are gone, and Marcie was right. I am all alone, but not without a fight.* Angie thought.

Calls to Frank for explanation were ignored; visits to his office were blocked. Soon smirks and laughter became apparent in his voice. "How could you treat me like this, Frank? I'm your wife," Angie would tell him.

In due time, Frank's deception and cunning ways angered Angie; her heart began to harden, her tears dried up, and her mind was filled with thoughts of resentment and punishment. It was time to take action. Her first thought was of killing him, but that seemed too easy. Also, taking his life would also take away hers, and Angie was not willing to give Frank any more of herself, not even in his death. At this point, Mitch seemed to play an extremely important role in everyone's life. It seemed Mitch's hopes and dreams for life, all his ambitions and failures, had somehow planted themselves in Angie's family. Frank seemed to have lost his own identity once he had possession of Turn it Up Productions. Mitch was Sharay's father; no matter how badly Angie wanted to ignore it, Mitch definitely was deceitful. She had to be smart; what better way to learn about a deceptive man than to learn from another deceptive man? Angie went to the very person that would understand her plight.

"Hello, Mitch," Angie said, uncomfortable because she had not seen Mitch since Sarah's death.

"Well, hello … Angie. What brings you to this dark and gloomy place?" Mitch questioned.

"Mitch, I know I should have brought Sharay to you a long time ago," Angie said, trying to justify her inattentive ways.

"Speaking of Sharay, why am I looking at you, Angie, and not my daughter? Where is Sharay?" Mitch questioned.

"She's in New York, Mitch, with Marcie and Frank. I know I should have brought her to you a long time ago, but …"

"But, but what, Angie? Why are you here? Is something wrong with Sharay? Is she hurt? What Angie, why are you sitting here mumbling to me? Is something wrong with my daughter?" Mitch questioned Angie coldly.

"No, Mitch. No, there's nothing wrong with Sharay. I'm here because I need your help. Frank has taken the girls with him to New York, and he won't give them back. He has my baby, Mitch; he has my baby, and I don't know how to get her back." Angie began to break down and cry.

"What, there in New York?" Mitch questioned, now puzzled about Angie's visit.

"Mitch, please, just listen to me for a minute. Frank has taken the girls to New York; he did it right after their graduation. He's somehow convinced Marcie to hate me, and I don't know why," she continued, speaking as she cried.

Mitch sat back in his cold, steel chair; he frowned as he tried to put Angie's visit and her distress together. "Oh … now I get it. Things not so sweet at home? My money wasn't enough for the two of you to stay together? But now you decide it's time to talk to me when it involves your daughter. Is that how it goes, Angie? You know what I mean; when it's your family, Angie, that's when it's important enough to come and see me. I look at you and I get sick."

"You get sick looking at me? You know what? I knew it was a

mistake to come here, Mitch. Who the hell do you think you are?" Angie said as she nervously picked up her things to leave.

"I'm asking you the same goddamned question, Angie. Where is my daughter? All this time I've sat here waiting to hear from either one of you, and all you can do is come to me sobbing because you've been betrayed by your precious husband. I trusted the both of you with my child, my child, Angie."

"What are we screaming about, Mitch, your child or your company? Don't try to play self-righteous with me. I've cared for that child when you couldn't recognize her as a breathing being. It was your company you loved, not Sharay. I wanted to let you know what was going on in her life, but her disgust for you was so strong I thought I would lose her if I did so. I wasn't going to let that happen. I had already lost her mother," Angie said as her eyes enlarged with anger. "What happened to my friend, huh Mitch, answer that? Where is she? Dead, Mitch. Is that because of your hands, Mitch? Do you have any idea of what I went through, not knowing if you killed my friend or not?

"I didn't; I didn't kill her." Mitch reacted.

If you didn't kill her with your hands, you killed her dreams and her desires. I know you beat her. Do you know that? Do you know that I know you put your hands on her for no reason except the guilt you felt about your lies and your cheating?"

"I know, I know," Mitch remorsefully replied.

"She gave you her all and still loved you. You tried to kill everything about her; would it be so hard to believe you killed her body?"

"No! No! No!" Mitch screamed. "I didn't kill her," he insisted, pounding his hand on the table and silencing Angie with his plea. "I did not kill her. You have to believe me; somebody has to believe me. I didn't kill my wife. I loved her," he said as he began to weep.

Tears of the sorrow of a weeping man fell from his face. Mitch's cry had a deep desperation in it. He wanted someone to believe him. Could it be true? Was there a possibility his forceful ways had filled him with the debt of guilt? As hard as it was for Angie to believe his cry of despair, to believe that maybe Mitch was telling the truth, she couldn't let these thoughts distract her. Finding the truth behind Sarah's murder was not the reason she was there. She needed to get her children back.

Frank had shown long ago his distaste for Angie; he was caught up in a world that did not belong to him. Angie needed Mitch's help. Could they both see past their anger and rescue the girls?

Marcie and Stephanie were overly excited about their trip to New York, and as Frank had promised, singers and musicians were needed for an upcoming occasion. It was a charity fundraiser to raise money for the needy. Well-known artists and musicians had shown up to support the charity. But to Marcie and Stephanie, it didn't matter who the show was for; this was their chance. As for Sharay, she could not forget Angie, who had been in her life since before the death of her mother. Maybe she had not shown her just how much she really loved her. Maybe Sharay didn't realize how much she loved her until now. Somehow, this was becoming more of a reality to Sharay.

Sharay looked around at what her father had built; there were pictures hanging on the walls by famous artists, rewards given to him for the work he had done to make other artis famous. One of the workers stopped to show interest in the admiring viewer. "May I help you?" he asked.

"Uh … no," she answered. "I'm just looking around."

"You're one of the newcomers, aren't you?" the young man asked.

"Yeah, you could say that," Sharay answered.

"You know, this side of the building is off limits to everyone," he stated.

"Oh yeah … so … what are you doing here?" Sharay questioned.

"Good question, but actually, I followed you down here, not really sure of what your intentions were."

"Oh, I see. You're the policeman of the company."

"Something like that," he said, blushing at the words Sharay spoke. "So … What do you do, dance or sing?"

"Actually, I do both, but my first love is singing," Sharay answered.

"So you're here for the charity event?"

"Yes I am; is there something else going on here?" Sharay asked.

"Oh yeah, there's always something going on here; there's an audition coming up for a play that's coming here in a few months." He told her that singers and dancers would be needed, and they continued to talk as he escorted Sharay back to the studio.

Marcie and Stephanie adjusted very quickly to the city's fast pace. It wasn't quite that way for Sharay. She saw for the very first time what her father had built. She was amazed by his surroundings and all the respect that people still had for him. The attitude of his employees showed in their disbelief that her father had had anything to do with the death of her mother. It puzzled Sharay, and it also made her question herself.

Could I have been wrong concerning my father? Why is it that everyone loves him so much? I don't understand. Sharay began to search her thoughts, *Who is this man that they speak of?*

Daily, Sharay would walk through the halls of Turn it Up Productions, trying to get a feel for what it was like to have been here when her father owned the company. Even though many years had passed, his presence was not erased. Not even Frank, who was accepted by Mitch loyal employees, was recognized as owner of this magnificent company. *Somehow I don't think Frank recognizes that,* she giggled to herself. As Sharay searched for answers, she decided to rest in one of the offices that was there when Mitch was in charge of the company. No one came in this part of the building other than to clean, so she was told. It was peaceful and silent, a place apart from everyone else.

"You're Sharay, aren't you?"

Sharay quickly turned around to face the young man who had spoken, very surprised by his presence. "Yes, I am Sharay," she politely answered the gentleman.

"Hi. I know who you are; my name is Tommy. How are you holding up? This is hard for you, isn't it? In a way no one would really understand."

"Yeah, I guess you're right. How long have you been standing there?" Sharay questioned.

"Not long," Tommy answered, "I was just admiring your strength."

"There's no strength here; I just continue doing what needs to be done. That's the story of my life. Can I ask you something?"

"Sure, anything," Tommy answered.

"Did you know my father?" Sharay questioned.

"Yes, I did. As a matter of fact, I knew your father very well. You know, your father was a brilliant man. It's so hard to believe, well ..."

"I know. I hear all the people talking, especially when they see me. They know I accused him of killing my mother."

"Well, I guess we all have to understand there are things you know that we don't. I just wish Mitch and Donna had looked more into the threat Brian made. You know, someone really did beat your father that night."

"What?" Sharay asked in response.

"No, it's true," Tommy continued.

"Well, why didn't someone come forward?"

"I don't know. I can't explain it. I've run it over again and again in my mind, but I can never come up with a clear answer. But I did the same thing with you; I wondered how you were doing, what you looked like, and how well you had grown, but I never went to find out," he told her.

"You know, this is hard. I look at my father's things and I find out that he was a brilliant man. I used to sit back and wonder what it was about him that even attracted my mother to him. Now, more and more, I can see what it was. And it's so sad to say, but it hurts to know he was somebody."

"Don't cry, Sharay." Tommy pulled her close into his arms. "You were young, and this was not your fault. Come on, girl, let me get you out of here. Come with me; I would like to show you how to take the anxiety you're feeling and turn it into … well, let me show you."

Tommy and Sharay entered one of the studio's dance halls and he began to show her some of the dances steps that were in the up-coming play the girls were supposed to dance in.

Life had already sunk its teeth into Sharay; maybe Tommy did have the right idea, and she should try dancing her way out of life's troubles.

Marcie had changed and was strange, while Stephanie was still trying to hold on to their promise of friendship. Stephanie had met a few new friends that loved to party and wanted Stephanie to come along; Stephanie agreed, and she asked Sharay to come and join in the fun. Sharay was so lost in her own troubles that she refused to go with Stephanie. After pleading with Sharay again, trying to get her to see she had to move on with her life, Stephanie gave up. Stephanie decided to go on without Sharay. She knew she could not continue to wait for her; it seemed like Sharay would never come.

So Teki became Stephanie's new friend. After several movie dates, they decided to go to an honorary party that was being given for Frank. On their drive to the party, Teki made Stephanie aware of a project Teki was interested in. He wanted to know if Stephanie wanted to come along. "Check this out," Teki said. "I have something I've wanted to show you ... but I was not sure how you would take it."

"What do you mean?" Stephanie inquired.

"Well ... look, I can show you better than I can talk about it. You've been telling me of how you needed more money, and fast, because of the condition your father is in back in Youngstown."

"Yeah ... ," Stephanie answered slowly.

"I have something for you right here that will change all of your money problems," he said as he pulled out a little brown jar.

Stephanie burst out laughing. "What's that, a little jar of hope?"

"No silly, I'm serious. This jar right here—what's inside will change all of your money problems, and you'll never have to worry about your father's financial problems again." Teki was persistent.

"Now you have my attention," Stephanie said as her eyes widened.

"In your area, where you live, Youngstown: it's the marketplace. It's one of a kind; it's the mob's meeting place, a playground per say," Teki continued.

"Come on, now," Stephanie said, smacking her lips. "How am I supposed to get this to Youngstown?"

"Girl, all you have to do is tell me you're willing to do this, and I'll take care of the rest. Are you in?" he asked, holding his hand out for Stephanie to take it in agreement. Stephanie rested her hand in his, astounded by the offer just given to her.

The closing of the steel mills had set the grip of poverty on the city of Youngstown. And the popularity of free-based cocaine was taking over at an alarming rate. As with everything else, it was divided into two groups: the sellers and the buyers. Stephanie had made the decision; her father was going to have enough money at last. So she made her connection with Teki. This, in turn, connected her to Brian and his wealth. Youngstown began to fill its wounds of poverty with the sap of cocaine, "the rich man's high," they called it.

Rumors that people were free-basing cocaine spread throughout the neighborhood. "Ed is smoking cocaine," they would say. "David is smoking cocaine; I heard Keisha is smoking cocaine. No … not Keisha!" All those interested in making fast money now had a quick way to make it: cocaine.

The sellers' pockets became full of mama's money, because the smokers robbed everyone they could to get money to buy the drug. "Give me your paycheck so I can get high," they demanded. "It's all about me," they said as the drug pounded through their veins.

The prosperous dealers set themselves up as kings of the city. They became rich off of the addicted. Their appearance changed from the power of the drug: their clothing and cars improved. They went from driving loud, rusty bottomed cars to driving the best looking vehicles in town. Gold was draped everywhere, from the wheels of the wealthy to the necks of the people. Jewelry was a key sign that prosperity had shined its light on them. The gold knots of jewelry they wore somehow made them believe that God Almighty had blessed them. Large, fourteen carat gold earrings were worn, two to three sets in each ear, and people wore rings on every finger. This finery represented how "the rich man's high" had brought riches to their lives, even though this richness was a lie. The truth was that idolatry had set up its throne, and all those involved in the drug trade were worshipping the calf of gold. Cocaine had become the god of Youngstown.

Stephanie needed this newfound wealth to help her father. And it did help. She allowed her father to believe it all came from Turn It Up Productions. Stephanie had gone to Sharay, explaining to her that she had not left her, that she was taking care of business, and that she was ok.

Sharay knew she had to find answers about who Brian was. She could not believe that everyone had loved her father so much, yet no one had done anything to save him. And from what Tommy had told her, Donna was the one who had the answers.

"Hello, Donna," Sharay said as she entered Frank's office.

"Hello, Sharay. You're as beautiful as everyone said."

"Thank you."

"Would you like to have a seat?" Donna said as she opened the silver streamline case that held her cigarettes. "You don't mind my smoking, do you?"

Sharay's innocence allowed her to speak quickly and still softly: "No. Oh no, I don't mind."

"I've been expecting you. I knew sooner or later you would come." The fire from Donna's lighter torched and lit the-long stemmed cigarette that hung from the side of her mouth. "Have a seat," she stated, directing Sharay with the wave of her hand. Sharay's heart fluttered at the sound of Donna's voice, not knowing what she might say next. Examining Donna's bold, cold structure, Sharay realized that she had not expected this. She had imagined Donna differently, maybe as a softer, more profound woman. *I came here thinking I may have caught Donna off guard, but instead, Donna has me scared and puzzled,* Sharay thought to herself. She decided to take Donna's invitation to sit down, and she did rest herself in the comfort of the chair that sat in front of Donna's desk.

Donna sat down too and began to talk about the reason she felt Sharay had come. "I'm quite sure you're here for answers concerning your father's affair with me."

Affair! You had an affair with my father? Sharay's thoughts stormed with fury as she heard the words coming from Donna's mouth. She pictured herself immediately jumping out of the chair she had just relaxed her body on, diving onto Donna, and beating the life out of her. Instead, she sat there. Anxiety rippled through her body as sweat beads formed along her nose. Donna continued to speak, telling of the love-making affair she seemed to enjoy so much while Sharay sat there, soaking up every word that came out of her mouth.

Was there any decency in this woman? Did she realize who she was talking to? I'm the daughter of the man you had this stinking affair with, you stinking skeezer. "I can't take anymore of this," she said as she ran out of the office.

Minutes later, Tommy entered Donna's office and questioned her to see if she had spoken to Sharay about Mitch getting beaten.

"Oh no … I thought … never mind, I have to catch her." Disheartened about the way she had reacted to Sharay, Donna grabbed her purse and keys, ran out of the office, and raced to catch up with Sharay. Needing very badly to explain herself, she knocked on Sharay's apartment door. "Sharay, please let me in," Donna begged, knowing now that her conversation with Sharay had been unfair.

Sharay demanded that Donna leave immediately, but Donna insisted that she needed to explain her conduct.

"I knew something was wrong at home. Sarah and Mitch were not getting along, and I knew that I was part of the reason," Donna began to explain. "I thought I could break Mitch away from Sarah with my love. But Mitch's love for Sarah was strong. I don't believe anyone could have ever gotten him away from her. Sarah was a different type of woman: a godly woman, a special woman. Mitch knew of the Lord, but he had not turned his life over to God. God was only something he needed in small increments. I loved the Lord; I loved your father more and I needed him in my life."

"What, and you expect me to pity you?" Sharay said, dismissing Donna's excuses.

"No, Sharay, I want you to hear me. You're a young lady growing into a beautiful woman; you need to hear these words, "One day, when you fall in love, these words may help you, Donna continued.

"Oh. What now, you're playing the mother's role?" Sharay before you turn me away, I need to tell you that there was someone very angry with your father and me. He wanted more than he ever should have had. He and his group should have never made it to the charts. His name is Brian; you know the group, LB?"

"What are you talking about? That is one of the best bands going," Sharay acknowledged.

"Yes, but not by their own doing," Donna answered. "They came to your father with demands. Listen to me, Sharay; they wanted us to book gigs that the group didn't have the talent for. We refused, but they had a contract. So then Tommy came along."

"Tommy," Sharay responded, shocked at hearing Tommy's name mentioned in this conversation. "What the heck is going on around here?"

"Sharay, you're not listening to me. Tommy wanted to move up in the company. Mitch had come back to New York, to the office. He had had an awful fight with Sarah and felt that no matter what he did, he would not be able to repair the damage he had done. He lost all hope and went on a drinking spree. I had to run the business myself. Mitch was gone longer than I thought he would be, and everything became too heavy, so I had other people working in the company to help me. You have to understand, your father knew what he was doing with this company. So I gave Tommy instructions to go and listen to this band, Brian's band, and told him to sign them on if they were good. They were right there in the city of Youngstown; we had gotten groups from there before which were tremendous, but not this one."

"What is your point?" she shouted, trying to carry the weight of Donna's words.

"Brian sent out serious threats. Threats that if he didn't get what he wanted, harm would come to Mitch. Mitch was not a fearful man, so he ignored the threats. The night before the tragedy, Mitch was jumped and beaten. The next day, your mother was killed."

"What? You're telling me my father was telling the truth, and no one came to his defense? No one helped him. What kind of people are you? Get the Hell out of here, Donna; get out before I throw you out!" Sharay demanded. "Why, why wouldn't you help my father?" she cried. Sharay fell to her knees, trying to bring all of the confusion together. *Why didn't someone help my father? All the years that I have accused him; he'll never forgive me.*

Repentance came into Donna's heart, and she fell to her knees, pleading for Sharay to forgive her.

Sharay decided to go home right away, and she took a bus to Youngstown immediately. Once there, she called Angie. She needed to hear her voice very badly. "Angie, hi," she said. Sharay broke down and began to cry.

"Sharay," Angie responded, full of the anxiety of not knowing if the girls were all right or not. "Are you all right? Is Marcie with you? Is Marcie all right? Let me speak to Marcie."

"Angie … Angie, she's not here. She's not here, Angie," Sharay sadly responded, knowing how badly Angie needed to speak to her daughter.

"Sharay, where are you? Where is Marcie? Oh my God, is everyone all right?" Angie began to cry. "Sharay are you there?" Angie questioned, anxiously waiting for answers.

"Yes, Angie. I'm here. I'm so sorry for the way we left, Angie."

"Sharay, how is my baby?"

"She's changed, Angie. But we're all okay. Angie, can I come home?" Sharay asked.

"Yes! Yes! Baby, where are you?" Angie questioned, relieved that she would see at least one of her children again.

"I'm at the bus station downtown."

"I'm on my way," Angie said and hung up the phone. She rushed out to meet Sharay. Their embrace was long and heartfelt. Apologies and acceptance filled the air. Upon returning home, Sharay began to give Angie insight into what she had seen on her visit to Turn it Up Productions. She explained to Angie that Marcie had made new friends, and how she had changed, and no longer wanted to be a part of her and Stephanie's sisterhood. She also described the way Marcie spoke about the company as if it belonged to her father and she had no regard for Sharay's feelings. But in all of that, there was still something very different about Marcie that she could not explain.

"Angie, I hate to sound like I don't care about what's going on with Marcie. But I spoke with a guy who said my father really did get attacked that night, and he doesn't know why no one stood up for my dad. He also stated that there's a man by the name of Brian who made repeated threats against my father and Donna, the young lady that was my father's secretary at the time. Both Donna and my father ignored his threats. I went to Donna to see if the story had any merit; I was trying to be an adult, all grown-up and able to handle the situation, to find some answers. But instead of her telling me anything about my father being beaten, she began to tell me about their fantastic love affair. Oh my God, I just couldn't take anymore, so I ran out of her office. Well, I guess guilt caught up with her." Sharay began to rock back and forth as she continued to explain to Angie what had happened. "Donna came running over to my apartment, telling me that it was true, that someone really had beaten my father the day before my mother was killed. I don't understand these people. I accused my father of killing my mother, and he was telling the truth. What am I going to do? How could he ever forgive me?"

Sharay sat on the side of the bed weeping tears of sorrow. Emotions haunted her as she thought about the death of her mother and the accusation she made against her father regarding her mother's death. Now she had found out she may have been wrong all along. She sat there twirling the slim, silver cigarette case that Donna had left in her apartment. Angie sat on the side of the bed with Sharay, to comfort her, maybe to comfort them both. She saw the silver case's reflection, and asked Sharay where she got the cigarette case from. Sharay explained that it was the case Donna had left in her apartment when she came with her awful story.

Angie's reaction to the cigarette case was a little different than Sharay's. This cigarette case strongly resembled the same case Frank had bought Angie as a gift shortly after their marriage. It was the same color and had the same design. But the case had been missing for awhile, almost forgotten by Angie until tonight. Without hesitation, Angie opened the cigarette case, hoping not to find the engraving that was now staring her right in the face. *Frank, Angie thought, you dirty dog.*

"Do you want to visit your father?" Angie asked Sharay.

"Yes," Sharay answered. "I guess it's time."

"Yes, I think it's time for me to make a few visits myself."

Angie pulled out her suitcase and began packing clothing needed for a trip, possibly a long one. Upon arriving in New York, Angie's first visit was to Donna.

"Okay Donna, it's time to get to the bottom of some things," Angie said as she closed Donna's office door. "You've dealt with a child; now let's take care of this, woman to woman." Angie continued speaking as she threw the cigarette case onto Donna's office desk.

Donna, surprised by Angie's unannounced visit, glanced down at the cigarette case sitting right below her nose. Lifting her head, she thanked Angie for bringing the case back to her.

"And I suppose you want to thank me for the use of my husband too. What is it with women like you?" Angie inquired. "First Sarah's husband and now mine, or is this your way of being an asset to the company?"

"Well, you know what they say: if you knew how to keep your man in his own bed, he wouldn't be sleeping in mine," Donna coldly answered.

"No, what you need to remember is to keep your legs closed and find your own man. It's called respect, but I can see you know nothing of that," Angie answered, recognizing what type of women she was dealing with.

"What do you want, Angie?"

"I want my daughter. That's what I want and I'm going to get it. You know I have to hand it to you, Donna; you are a cold woman. How could you stand back and just watch a family be torn apart like this?"

"Why are you acting so brand new Angie?" Donna questioned. "You know the story: while the cat's away, the mice will play. That's your family, so it's your responsibility. If you can't keep it together, someone else will."

"It's like that, huh, Donna?" Angie charged, stepping up to her, "but guess what: I'm not going to give you that pleasure. If you want him, you can have him. I didn't come here for Frank. I came for my daughter."

While Donna and Angie were arguing, Frank entered Donna's office expecting to go over some papers. But upon seeing Angie, his disposition changed greatly. He asked Angie why she was there and demanded that she leave.

"Uh … now you show up. You mean all I had to do was approach your precious Donna? I woke up, Frank. I walked through the front door," Angie said, arguing.

"I don't want you, Angie. You're nothing but a hindrance to me; the love I had for you is dead and gone. Nothing about you represents who I am now," Frank announced boldly, full of conceit.

"Well, thank you Frank, I can handle that coming from the likes of you. At least you finally manned up and told me to my face. Now let me tell you, I wasn't a weak woman when you met me, and I won't be one now. I helped carry this family—or did you forget? What broke me was the way you did things. You have no respect, Frank. You have no respect for me as a woman. I am the woman who gave birth to your only child. What is wrong with you? You can fall out of love with me, but did you have to become my worst enemy? And you actually find peace in taking my child from me? You've been ignoring all of my calls. You won't receive any of my visits, and you took my daughter away from me without telling me even one reason why. And now the best thing you can say to me is to get out of here? Where is my daughter, or are you not even man enough to tell me that?"

"Angie, I want you out of here now!" Frank demanded.

"Let me make this perfectly clear to the both of you. I'm not going anywhere. I'll be right across the hall. You see Frank; I have just as much right to this business as you do."

"You know nothing about this business," Frank said, doubting her ability to manage a company.

"What do you think you can run around here?" Donna said as she smirked and giggled, drawing deeply on a cigarette.

"That's why I have the two of you," Angie responded. "You can run the business. I'll just sit back and watch. Oh, and I have something even better for you, Donna. The next time you decide to buy a car, buy it in your own name. I'll be driving the Porsche; your new set of car keys are in the Chevy parked around back—how did I handle that?" she asked, walking out of the office.

Angie had set a spark of fury in Frank, and there was nothing he could do about it. She was right. Mitch had left both Angie and Frank in charge of Sharay's estate. At this point, the only thing Frank could do was retreat, and Angie knew it. Angie decided to make the back staircase her entrance; it was a much better way to approach the building; no one would know the exact time when she would arrive. She could see that Frank had a deep dislike for her. What Frank didn't realize was that the feeling went both ways. Still, caution was the best tactic. So as part of her daily routine, she took the back staircase, arriving at a different time each day.

On one particular day, Angie decided to go into work much earlier than usual. As she walked up the staircase, close to Donna's office, she could hear a man's voice speaking on the way out of Donna's office. He stood in front of her office door and reminded her of the favor he had done for her, and he added that he didn't need Donna to let him down. The money was needed. Donna encouraged the man not to worry and said that she had everything taken care of, but she needed him to leave before someone would see him. Angie quickly hid herself in the corner of the staircase, trying not to be seen. But to her surprise, the front door wasn't this man's first preference either. As the man passed Angie and politely greeted her with a "good morning," she realized she had seen him somewhere before. Not able to place where, Angie continued on with her day. She was very suspicious of what she had seen and heard.

Marcie, Stephanie and Sharay had put their all into the charity show, and it worked. Frank recognized the girls' talent and regretted that he hadn't let them perform sooner. *It was a good thing no one else found them.* Now it was all up to him to make the best of their talent.

Frank started to structure their career. He decided to place the girls with two young men he knew who would perfect their song and dance moves for the up-coming play. Frank knew now more than ever that he was a lucky man to have all of this fall into his hands. But gratefulness was something Frank seemed to have forgotten; somehow he felt he had created the business all on his own. Where did all of this arrogance come from: money, power, or insecurity? His former insights about his daughter were totally lost. Frank gave her the kind of freedom that was not good for any child. He trusted her friends to care for her, knowing she knew nothing of city life. Frank had not taken notice of the dark circles that surrounded Marcie's eyes or the weight loss she had experienced. She'd tell him she was dieting, and he would believe her. Without taking a deeper interest in her life, Frank was content just in knowing that he had taken Marcie from Angie.

But not Angie: she knew something was wrong with her baby. She had changed so much. Her love for her mother was gone, but something else was wrong with Marcie. Angie had to figure it out; there was too much weight loss, and there were too many colds. *What is going on with my baby?* It was good to see Marcie, whether she appreciated it or not. Frank had gotten her an opening for one of the groups' concerts. Marcie could not even manage to show up for that. Angie thought that Frank would have tried to find out why she did not remember. But no ... he was able to fill the spot with a stand-by, and that was good enough for him. It showed that he had power to handle anything and everything that could come up.

The company was beautiful, full of color and bright-minded people. As Sharay had said, Mitch was most alive in the presence of the people; the respect they had for him was spoken of daily. It was so strange that no one spoke up for Mitch, if he really had been beaten.

One night after rehearsal, Angie and Sharay sat watching television when the evening news came on. It showed the interview of a police officer in Youngstown. He talked about the different signs you could use in order to determine if your child or anyone else was on drugs. He was with the prevention center and was trying to help those who had fallen into the trap of drugs. Angie almost choked on her popcorn when she realized that this officer was the same man that was at Donna's office door. And now, dressed as a police officer, she recognized him as Officer Brown. And as much as Angie did not want to admit it; she also recognized some of the drug signs in Marcie that this officer Brown was speaking of. So Angie made the trip to Youngstown, hoping that her insight was wrong.

It was difficult returning to a home she had not been in for months. It was empty and cold. Angie's thoughts raced back to the day when the house was full of joy and noise. She remembered the excitement she felt when she knew her husband was on his way home. She remembered the joy she felt when she saw Marcie stumble after learning to take her first steps. She remembered that Marcie had been trying to get to her father as he entered the door after a long day at work. And now she was trying to find a way to save her baby from a great hazard.

"Hi Officer Brown" Angie said, greeting the officer after her long trip home.

Officer Brown was flattered that Angie had seen him on television and had come from so far away to speak with him. He informed her of all the signs she needed to watch for, making her fully aware that she had a long journey ahead of her. But, thank God, Marcie was not free-basing. That had become a serious problem in the nation and in Youngstown especially. Angie was very appreciative of the help Officer Brown had given her and for his patience. But then she let him know that she recognized him because he was working on her friend's case. "Your friend?" he replied.

"Yes," Angie said. "You were one of the officers who worked on the case of Sarah, Sarah Turner; she was my friend, my best friend."

"Ma'am, I have worked on many cases here in the Youngstown area," Officer Brown answered.

"I'm sure you have," Angie replied. "But I'm sure you would remember her. Her name was Sarah, Sarah Turner; she was murdered about twelve years ago. Do you remember her?"

The officer gave a little smirk and stated that they had so many cases in the city that he was not quite sure about which one Angie was referring to. In the same breathe he quickly brushed Angie off.

"That was strange, "Angie thought.

Angie did not know where to go with the hunch she felt, so it was time to play a guessing game. Straight to the telephone booth she went.

"Donna."

"Yes, Angie."

"Donna, I want you to meet me in Chinatown tomorrow at lunch time."

"And why should I meet with you anywhere, Angie?" Donna questioned.

"Would the name Officer Brown help you any, Donna?"

As Angie requested, Donna did show up at lunch time. *So now what am I to do?* Angie pondered. "Here, we'll sit here at this table," Angie instructed the waitress. Donna's only request was for an ice tea. Angie knew she had to say something.

"Okay, Angie, I'm through playing your game. Quit wasting my time," Donna advised, bothered by Angie's agitating ways.

"You know, Donna, it puzzled me that you would show up here just because I mentioned Officer Brown's name. Are you having a fling with Officer Brown? Is this something Frank should know about?"

"You know what Angie, just as I figured, you don't know what you're talking about."

"Oh no? Then why did I see Officer Brown leaving your office early in the morning? Do you think there's something you need to tell me?" Angie asked, filled with interest.

"Why would I need to reveal anything to you, Angie?" Donna said, getting up from the table. "Oh, before you run back filling Frank's head with one of your jealous accusations, Officer Brown is not my creep, he's my brother." And she turned and walked away.

"Your brother?" Bewildered, Angie tried to figure out their connection. "Well, one thing I can say for the both of them. They both are acting very strangely. Someone is hiding something."

One particular day, while Sharay was searching through her father's things, she decided to play some of the old music Mitch had in his office. The music began to play, and Sharay sat back in a chair to relax. The music continued on for a few minutes, and then the singer broke his words down into a threat. Stating that he was speaking to Mitch, he said that if Mitch did not get them the gigs they had asked for, Mitch would feel the consequences. The threats were just as Tommy had said. Sharay pulled the eight-track from the player and ran to Angie. Upon entering Angie's office, she found two officers there with Angie talking about Sarah's death.

"Angie, you need to hear this," Sharay said as she hurried into Angie's office so fast that she did not recognize the two police officers standing there.

"Wait, Sharay," Angie requested. "These two officers wish to talk about Sarah's case; it's been re-opened."

"I know, Angie; I re-opened it," Sharay stated. "Hi, how are you?" Sharay was polite to the officers.

"I'm sure you remember me," Officer Brown said to Angie.

"Yes, I do remember you Officer Brown."

"And how is your daughter?" he curiously questioned her.

"The same," Angie replied. "Officer Brown, it would be better if we meet with you at the police station."

"Is there a reason why, ma'am? Is there something you need to let us know?" Officer Brown asked.

"I have something for you," Sharay stated.

"No, Sharay. We'll talk to the police officers at the police station," Angie insisted.

Sharay deeply wanted to tell the officers what she had found, but Angie kept cutting her off every time she began to speak. "Like I said, Officer Brown," Angie began to say, "I haven't been here at the company long, but if there's anything you need, I am willing to help.

"What is wrong with you, Angie? I was trying to give the officers this tape," Sharay said as she tried to understand Angie's actions.

"What is that?" Angie questioned.

"Listen." The music stopped and the threats began.

Angie quickly stopped the music player. "We can't listen to this here; meet me at my apartment."

And so they did. Angie and Sharay both met at Angie's apartment while Angie explained to Sharay that she did not want Officer Brown to learn anything of what they may have learned. From now on, they both needed to inform each other about what they found, no matter how unimportant it seemed. Angie told Sharay that not only was Officer Brown the officer who worked on Sarah's case twelve years ago, but he was also Donna's brother.

"Donna's brother! What is going on here? First we have a tape with the threats to Mitch on it, and now the officer who worked on my mother's case is the brother of the woman my father was having an affair with. I'll kill them!" Sharay exclaimed.

"I don't know how to piece this together yet, but there's a whole lot more going on here than what meets the eye," Angie responded.

"It's obvious; Donna probably had my father beaten. Oh my God, she may have had my mother killed." Sharay jumped up, on her way to confronting Donna.

"Wait. Wait, Sharay. We don't have enough proof. If you go over there now and reveal what we already know, they'll be able to hide what we don't know," Angie insisted.

"I'll kill her; I'll kill her, Angie," Sharay said as she fought against the air and then burst into tears.

"Just wait, baby; we'll work together. Just stay with me," Angie said, grabbing Sharay and trying to help her get in control of her rage.

So Angie went to Tommy and questioned him about the Brian who had threatened Mitch. Tommy knew quite a bit of information. He gave all he could in order to try to help the case. But the same story kept coming up. "Donna sent me to Youngstown; she set up a meeting with this guy, Brian.I was supposed to listen to his band and sign a contract with the band if they were good enough. The band ended up not sounding good at all, and I refused to put them on our label. But Donna said, to give them the contract, that this Brian was a friend and that with enough work the band would make it. So I did; I didn't want to lose my job by not listening. Plus, there was a huge bonus in it for me. Why wouldn't I sign them on? That's all I had to do. Donna and Mitch handled the rest," Tommy answered.

Angie knew she had to talk to Brian to find out exactly what Donna had set up with him. *Was he responsible for the murder of my friend?*

Brian had become a great musician and song writer. His music had sold millions of records. His astonishing lyrics and the way his words fell together created emotions in people, and everyone tapped along to the beat. The band he had started with had fallen away, and Brian had gone through three other groups before he had reached his fame. His music had really taken off.

The one conclusion Angie came to was that she needed to figure out who had murdered her best friend. Officer Brown knew much more than he was willing to admit. The threats of this "Brian" constantly came up, and there was also a lot of talk about the mistress/secretary who needed the wife out of the way.

As time passed during their investigations, Stephanie had changed too. She was no longer the little girl Angie and Sarah knew and loved. She was hard and ruthless, flighty and bossy. But she knew Brian, perhaps a little too well for her own good. It was strange for the girls to lose themselves so easily. It was also strange to Angie that Marcie was able to find Stephanie but Sharay couldn't.

Angie had to follow Stephanie's guidance in order to get close to Brian. Stephanie had decided to introduce Angie as an anxious, up and coming movie producer. Brian had climbed the ladder and was willing to gain more fame and money. Angie had to get into character; she had pulled herself up from the heart-broken mom to become an outgoing, powerful movie producer. Acting out such a change in stature was overwhelming for Angie; no one had seen Angie so striking. She was ready. Angie knew everyone was tired of hearing her ask about the death of Sarah, but what else was she to do? Sarah had died a gruesome death. Why was her killer still unknown? "Dead and gone" was the phrase. There had to be a reason, an answer to her question. Why was Sarah taken away? Angie was determined to find out.

Stephanie set up a date and time for Brian and Angie to meet. The meeting went well. Brian really liked Angie, and he showed a lot of trust in what he believed she could do. She was fresh, exciting, and beautiful. Stephanie was amazed by Brian's response to Angie. She had never seen him react to a woman like that before. Stephanie, Angie, and Sharay had a lot of work ahead of them. Brian was told that he was needed to star as a new found dancer and that more meetings would be scheduled to bring the whole scene together if he was willing to play the part. Brian agreed.

Angie's powerful feelings of fury could not be hidden once she and Stephanie arrived back at Angie's apartment. Brian had walked away with the answers that she so deeply needed. Stephanie was relieved that things went as well as they did. Sharay was relieved that both of them were safe. Preparations had to be made. A dance studio and dancers were needed to complete the scene. These things could easily be acquired by Sharay. Since Angie had moved into her own office, Sharay was able to take over more of the business. Angie needed desperately to get closer to Brian, to find out what went on in his world. She thought of invitations to dinner and the idea of working her way into his life as an interesting female. It was possible, but it seemed like this idea would take too much time. Plus, Brian was a busy man himself, so what did he care about another female trying to get acquainted with him? No … Angie had to play it smart; things had to go lightly, and the best way for Angie to become close to Brian was by making her Brian's dance partner.

Brian was an excellent dancer and singer; the stage was nothing new to him. Angie had to be excellent just to keep up with him. She had danced years ago, but she had not been trained as well as Brain. Angie decided she had to change the dance style to modern dance, the rumba, or the cha cha, something that would take Brian out of his comfort zone. The idea was to make Brian work just as hard as Angie; that way the harder the dance, the longer they would have to practice. The time they spent together would give Angie the opportunity to get acquainted.

Difficulty came with each attempt Angie made to get closer to Brain. Angie first had to renew her dance moves practice. So the dance lessons began. Stephanie and Sharay joined in as part of the dance team, and they also brought Tommy in too. He could show all of them what they needed to know to perfect their skills. The reunion of the three brought back a togetherness that had long been forgotten. Laughter filled the room as Angie tripped over her own feet as she tried to stay in the rhythm of the dance moves.

It was funny; Angie was able to relate to Stephanie and Sharay so easily, but she was still rejected by her own daughter. *Was I that bad of a mother?* Angie thought.

After weeks of rehearsal, it was time to bring Brian in on the rehearsals. He had returned from a previous obligation and was ready to begin his journey with Angie. What Angie did not realize was that Brian was not as stupid as she wanted to believe. He was not willing to just accept a stranger into his life, even if she was beautiful, for that was not the way he operated. Brian had many illegal things going on in his life, things that he always thought of as his "fall back plan." After serious investigation, Brian found out that Angie was no more than a housewife. *What could she possibly want?* Brian speculated that maybe someone was using her as a way to get into his life and destroy it. And that "someone" could only be the cops. Brian played the game with Angie, thinking she was an undercover cop and that either Stephanie was too young to figure this out or that she had set him up. Brian was puzzled about why she would do something like that, but he knew he was not going down without a fight. No one anywhere had ever heard of Angie or knew of her up-coming movie. Brian played along with Angie's game; he was so tuned into her every move that he never let on that he knew she was not a movie producer.

Until one day Brian felt he had had enough. He and his boys dragged Marcie into the studio where Sharay, Stephanie, and Angie were all rehearsing. "Is this your daughter?" Brian ruthlessly demanded an answer to his question as he gripped Marcie by her hair.

"Yes. Yes," Angie fearfully answered, dropping the hot cup of coffee that was in her hands to the floor. "What are you doing with her?"

"What did you think, Angie: that you could just dance your way into my life and I would just fall for that silly bull? What kind of fool do you take me for? Huh?" Brian asked as he yanked Marcie's hair, moving her head with every angry word he spoke.

Marcie was in bad shape. She stood there pleading with Angie, begging her to tell Brian what was going on. She needed a hit bad, and Brian used every bit of her need to get the answers he wanted.

"So where's the big bust?" Brian questioned, demanding answers.

"Big bust? I don't understand. What big bust?" Angie courageously asked, trying to find out.

"Don't play stupid with me, Angie; I'm done playing your stupid game." One of Brain's chore boys walked up to Marcie and put a gun barrel to her head. The other one stepped up to Angie and ripped her blouse open. "Are you wired?" he asked. He had expected to find one under her shirt.

"No! No!" Angie screamed, folding her arms around her body and trying to cover herself. "What the Hell is this?" Angie asked, becoming angrier at Brian's disrespectful ways.

"Look, I don't know what's going on here," Marcie said. "But there's nothing my mother can do to you. She's only a secretary in my father's business."

"Your father's business," Sharay shouted, sick and tired of Marcie claiming what did not belong to her. "My father built that business, you dumb coke whore."

"Well, what the Hell is going on here?" Brian asked, not understanding Sharay's reaction.

"I'll tell you what's going on. You killed my friend, and I want answers about why you did it," Angie said.

"What are you talking about lady? I ain't killed anybody," Brian answered, defending his innocence.

"Sarah, Sarah Turner," Angie screamed, "you know who I'm talking about."

"Here we go again," Marcie said. "Gun to my head, this man wants to take my life, and what is the first name you holler? Sarah." Marcie placed her hands on her hips.

But just as fast as Marcie had flicked the words out of her mouth, Sharay dove straight on her and beat her to let her know that it was Sharay's mom Marcie seemed to be so disgusted with.

"She loved you, Marcie, how could you treat her so badly?" Sharay said as she pounded.

"Wait a minute," Brian said. "something is very wrong here. You're not the police?"

"No, we're not the police. I'm here to find out why you beat the life out of my friend. What did she do to you that you had to kill her?" Angie asked, courageously fighting for the answers regarding Sarah's death.

"Kill her? Look, I ain't killed anybody," Brian said, defending his innocence.

"Twelve years ago, Youngstown Ohio. The city's south side, Blue Buick. You didn't beat my friend until you split her skull open?" Angie asked.

"No, lady, I didn't," Brian said, proclaiming his innocence.

Angie insisted that she knew what she was talking about. "Are you telling me you weren't there?"

"Yes, I was there, a few of my friends and me. We were sent there to stir up some confusion, maybe scare her a little. But when we got there she was already dead. Someone had gotten there before us."

"No, she wasn't," Sharay said, jumping in. "I had just spoken to my mother and asked her if I could go bike riding. She was not dead. I saw you sitting in the back seat of your car."

She's right, Brian, I was with her," Stephanie exclaimed. "We saw you sitting in your blue car, like you were a gangster or something."

Marcie spoke up. "That's right. I was with them also. We saw you there."

"What? You're trying to tell me you didn't beat Sarah?" Angie asked. "Sarah had no enemies. We have your threats on tape; don't lie to me. Don't lie," Angie said, raising her voice as she sought the truth.

"You know, Angie, I don't like anyone questioning me. But out of respect for your friend, I will tell you that I did not kill your friend; someone had gotten to her before we did. But our plans were not to kill her, just to scare her," Brian explained, irritated by Angie's boldness.

"But how did you know her? She bothered no one. You had to learn where she lived from Mitch or Donna," Angie continued.

"Yes, you're right; all of our information came from a female. Now exactly who, I don't know. I haven't known all of these years. We were stopped by a police officer who seemed to know everything about us, including the threats we had made to Mitch at Turn it Up Productions. He told us if we didn't follow through with what he wanted done, he would arrest us for dealing drugs. He promised that he would make sure we went to jail. They just wanted her roughed up. Plus, there was a big bonus if we did exactly as they asked, and he said, no-one would bother us while we sold drugs in the Youngstown area. Money and freedom: how could you refuse an offer like that?" Brian asked as he concluded.

Brian felt it was time for him and his boys to drop out of sight. But just as they were trying to exit the room, Donna stepped in. She was armed with her gun. "I figured I'd save you the trouble of trying to find me. I knew the moment I saw you, Angie, that there was going to be a problem. Life works in the strangest ways. I loved Mitch. I watched him in pain and agony over Sarah. They weren't meant to be together. It was obvious that he belonged to me. But he kept on trying to rekindle their love. Finally, that last argument gave me the advantage I had looked for. It was as if God had given me a chance of a lifetime. God knew their marriage was over," Donna said. "I think I fell in love with God even more. The world became brand new. The sun was brighter, and nights were warmer. I did nothing to make Mitch leave Sarah, and that made me guilt free. It was a decision I had nothing to do with, so who could blame me? It should have happened a long time ago. I was high, high as the highest mountain; rainbows danced all around me. God's promises had happened in my life. And then that day came again when Mitch started rejecting my love. He wanted his Sarah back, and he knew she was there waiting for him."

"You killed my mother," Sharay said, enraged.

"Shut up!" Donna said as she pointed the gun at Sharay.

"Mitch was going home again, to leave me again. He wanted to make his over-done marriage work. It was over, why couldn't he see that? But again, he wanted me to sit and wait on him. I wouldn't do it, not this time. Brian had come to the office threatening Mitch, and he wanted to bring those threats to Youngstown. Youngstown was a mob city, and everyone knew it. Officer Brown was very familiar with the crimes in the city, and he knew who was responsible for most of them. All he had to do was beat the crap out of Mitch the night before Mitch left to talk to Sarah. I would convince Mitch that the beating was God's way of telling him it was over between him and Sarah; I would tell him that the Lord did not want him to go back to her. It was a perfect plan, but the following morning she still won. The heifer went and got herself killed. I wasn't going to spend the rest of my life trying to convince Mitch that it wasn't his fault. When I heard Frank and Angie were to take over the business, I decided to stand my ground and keep my job.

Silence was my best tool; there was no way I was going to allow my brother's name to be involved in a murder he had nothing to do with. So I didn't speak up for Mitch. Hey, consequences can be more than one can bear," Donna said in conclusion as she tapped her slender cigarette on the handle of her gun.

"My God. Well, if you didn't kill Sarah, who did?" Angie asked.

"I did," Frank said as he walked into the room with his gun aimed directly at Angie.

"What!" Angie said as her heart dropped down into her stomach.

"I tried to talk to your father, Sharay, to get him to understand that he was no good for Sarah. Whatever love he had for her was lost. He wasn't able to love Sarah. I needed him to let her go. But he refused."

"What! Why? Why, Frank? Not you," Angie said tenderly.

Frank began to explain his theory that Angie was responsible for Sarah's death. He said that it was all her fault because she was the one who brought Sarah into their home. "I fell in love with her the very first day I met her," Frank explained.

Angie tried to understand Frank as the deceptive words fell from his lips and pierced her heart. He had already become a man she couldn't recognize. But the idea that he would murder Sarah had never crossed her mind.

"You brought her home, to our house, to our home." Frank continued, "if not for you, Angie, I would never have known her. Marcie would never have known her; I would never have fallen in love with her."

"What! Are you crazy?" Marcie asked, taking her mother's side.

"I heard you, Brian," Frank continued, ignoring Marcie. "I heard that you plotted to hurt Mitch. I knew they were going to take Mitch's life if they had to. I begged Mitch to let Sarah go, to give me a chance to love her, care for her, and show her what a real man was like. He just laughed at me and said, 'You, Frank? What are you going to do with

Sarah? Huh? Tell me Frank, what can you do with my baby? Oh my God. Does she even want you? Tell me she wants you, tell me she sent you here to ask me to let her go; can you tell me that?' I felt so stupid. Mitch had made a fool of me; I was so angry. I heard Brian and his boys make their plot, and I made them an offer. Brian knew me from the bank; he had tried several times to take out a loan at our bank, but he was refused each time. So I made him an offer: come to Youngstown, and I will guarantee that your loan application goes through. I was sick of Mitch; he had everything and appreciated nothing. Sarah was beautiful, a man's dream, and all Mitch did was mistreat her, spend money, and live a life that the average person doesn't get to live. He won in everything, even when it came to Sharay; you are as beautiful as your mother was. Sarah denied me time and time again. I loved you Angie. I never meant to fall in love with Sarah. I wasn't going to let you go until I knew you were okay with everything."

"Okay? How would I have possibly been okay with my husband living next door to me with my best friend? You're sick," she said.

Don't act like you never saw the way Mitch looked at you!" Frank screamed, losing control of his emotions. "Mitch wanted you and you know it."

"Mitch wanted everything. That was no secret. Frank, what happened to faithfulness, trust, and respect?" Angie asked spitefully.

"You don't understand; I loved Sarah just like I loved you," Frank continued. "I never meant to hurt her. She didn't understand. I went to her again to explain my love for her. She was in the kitchen cleaning up; Darin had gotten burned on the job again and they both were laughing and talking about his burns, I guess. It agitated me so badly just to see her laughing with another man. As I entered the kitchen, I asked Sarah if I could speak with her. I could tell she wanted to refuse, but Darin was willing to remove himself from the room. He stated he just got home from work and needed sleep. The situation was perfect for me. Sarah reluctantly said "okay." I began to pour my heart out to her. She just stayed busy cleaning up the cotton pads from Darin's injury. I only wanted her to stop what she was doing and listen to what I had to say; she seemed so aggravated. I had a plan, and it would have worked, but she loved you, Angie, and refused. Her words were as mean as Mitch's; I had never seen her like that before. 'Don't you know I love Angie?' she said. 'She's my friend. Do you understand the meaning of those words, Frank?' She questioned me as if I was a little boy, mocking me, and I couldn't take it. I grabbed her, but she fought me. Can you believe that, after all the hitting and beating she took from Mitch, but she fought back against me?? Mitch was the one she should have fought back against. I went crazy. I lost it. It was the last hit that brought me back, I could hear Sarah's head hit the edge of the table and I watched her fall to the floor. She was gone. What was I to do? I went to examine her when I heard Sharay calling her mother. I ran; I had to run," Frank said as he dropped his head. He had just confessed to the murder of Sarah Turner.

The room was quiet; no one said a word. Who would have thought it was Frank who took Sarah's life? Frank's greed and his desire for another man's world had taken away someone both innocent and beautiful. Even though Sarah and Mitch's marriage was not a perfect one, Frank had no right to try to step into Mitch's shoes. Suddenly, the sound of gun shots rang out in the room. The shot was fired by Marcie. "How could you?" she screamed. "You lied to me all of these years." The bullets hit Frank hard, and his body jerked as the bullets pierced him. "I suffered because of you," Marcie said. The last gun shot rang out, hitting Frank in the center of his chest. Frank dropped to the floor.

www.ingramcontent.com/pod-product-compliance
Lightning Source LLC
Chambersburg PA
CBHW021235280526
45784CB00005B/2104